ALIENS ANSWER

A telepathic call results in astounding,
beautiful, mind-bended conversations
with non-Earth beings

Mary Barr &
Steve Reichmuth

λ

Standing Wave Press

Cover by www.vedicdesign.com

Published in the United States of America

ISBN: **978-0-9895231-0-3**

First Edition

First Printing, 2013

To those who seek knowledge of the cosmos and non-Earth species through the understanding of and use of telepathy

Telepathy is a common and natural part of communication between many life forms. It has been tested and proven. It is nature's way of increasing survival through immediate thought contact. It is through this quantum-based means, mind-to-mind communication, that communication exists between more advanced species.

Examples of successful telepathic contact are abundant. Australia's Aborigines use telepathic contact in their practice of 'singing' someone home who has been on a 'walk about.' Astronaut Edgar D. Mitchell, a crewmember of the 1971 *Apollo 14* mission, did an experiment in telepathy with four people 150,000 miles below on the earth. To his pleasant surprise, two of his communicators responded with statistically significant success.

Considering the usefulness of telepathy, it should not surprise the reader that more advanced species have developed their telepathic abilities and use them extensively.

Table of Contents

FOREWORD

A telepathic message from Han, Zestra, and Gen, Zeta Reticulians:

This is an unusual book. There is great depth in what we have shared and explored together. This wonderful exchange that has occurred will continue. This is an ongoing open channel or avenue of communication that will continue beyond this book. We have been happy with our contacts with humans over the last several decades, yet we think it is necessary for a breakthrough that will deepen and broaden our relationship between your species and ours. We have reached a level of maturity where we think this is now appropriate. We have been frustrated with the lack of further integration of our presence into your society. This has been resisted or made secret. It is as if some humans wish to control the information of our presence, thus holding us back. We do not think that is right. We think that this book will help open up and break certain stereotypes about what you might imagine us to be.

We wish to create a feeling of well-being and comfort and give a friendly exchange of good wishes to show how we are different and how we are very much alike, in some ways. This is appealing to us and this book is to help facilitate that exchange. This is to give humanity some amazing insights into our culture and to share some of our science. We tactfully bring a certain degree of knowledge, which we share with you, without confining or restricting your ability to discover it yourselves. We indicate certain general directions to take, without necessarily providing detailed answers. This is to enable you to have the joy of discovery on your own. We try to provide a view of the Universe that is not Earth-centered.

Let it be known that life is everywhere. It is quite remarkable, and humanity is not separate from it. Humanity is both special and not special. Becoming aware of others in this very large and diverse family of life in the Universe will not diminish humanity. This is an important statement for humanity. Many worry about being diminished.

ACKNOWLEDGEMENTS

We are indebted to Han, Zestra, and Gen, who provided insights into their Zeta Reticulian culture. A special thanks to Jennifer for her editorial assistance. Love and appreciation to Lisa, who assisted in the final technical aspects of publication.

Sketch of Han from Zeta Reticuli
by Steve Reichmuth

ALIENS ANSWER

Session I, The Beginning
July 11, 2011

(Note: This is non-fiction. Questions are in italics. All answers are exact quotes, unless otherwise indicated.)

In the role of hypnotherapist, I regressed one of my clients several times to recall past life experiences. These retrievals were very successful. The client, Steve, requested that he be hypnotized in an attempt to talk to aliens. My reaction to his request was, 'Well, why not?' Steve, to the best of his knowledge, has never had a direct conversation with an alien. (Steve does have a retrieved memory of seeing an alien craft when he was a child. In addition, he has a childhood memory of a short being placing his arm around Steve's shoulder and leading him to a craft, but not inside.)

The therapist placed the client in a deep trance. The therapist asked, 'Are there any non-Earth beings (aliens) who are willing to make contact?' There was silence. The therapist suggested to Steve that his electrical field vibration was now raised by 30 per cent to facilitate contact. At this juncture, Steve started describing a small being, mostly hidden in shadows, who seemed to want to make contact. Upon my invitation to make contact, the being responded in a rather soft voice. Speaking through Steve, he said,

I am here.

Who are you?

You may call me Han.

Where do you come from?

Zeta Reticuli.

Startled, the therapist asks the contact, 'What is your agenda?'

To make contact.

Taken aback, therapist paused and then decided to investigate this entity by testing his knowledge by asking if he would answer some questions.

Yes.

Has Mars sustained any advanced life? (Test question.)

Not as you would think of life. It has grown lower-level algae type life. There are those who wish so much for there to be ancient and more advanced life on Mars that they misinterpret what they see as structures.

What is the function of dark matter? (Test question.)

Dark energy? It is a placeholder in the Universe.

Why are the galaxies in our Universe being pulled to one side? (Test question.)

It is just an impression that they are being pulled to one side. When compared to the entire Universe, they are not.

What is the shape of the Universe? (Test question.)

I am placing an image in Steve's mind. It is something like a cluster of bubbles.

Are there energy gestalts between planets/galaxies/Universes? (Test question.)

Yes and much more that could be seen as types of gestalts.

Why are you taking samples of humans, animals, and plants? (Test question.)

We do take samples, but our purpose is to perpetuate and seed other planets. We do not wish to cause harm. Sometimes, however, some lose their lives due to the stress of the process. We are rather like bees, moving life along.

What should we know about the bottom of our oceans and the species found there? (Test question.)

There are many life forms and they come and go from there.

Are there federations between planets/galaxies? (Test question.)

Yes.

Do members of your species have individual souls? (Test question.)

Yes.

Do you eat food? (Test question.)

Not food as you do, but primarily, we take on nourishment in a liquid form that fulfills all that we need.

Are there Universal laws? (Test question.)

Yes.

Is there one that prohibits one species from becoming so abundant that it overruns another? (Test question.)

Self-regulation. We maintain our population by regulating procreation.

Is there an appreciation of music with your species? (Test question.)

Ah! What better way to communicate! Yes, we do enjoy music, although it is different from your concept and experience of music.

Note: Thus ended the first session. Because of the interesting responses, the therapist prepared questions in advance for the next and all following sessions. Occasionally, a few others contributed questions: a science teacher, a medical doctor, and the client. These sessions were done with a single client. However, it became evident that Han, can and does come through others, if requested, with the same bright, diplomatic personality.

The source of most questions comes from this therapist's strong interest in science, medicine, history, psychology, spirituality, cultural anthropology, music, and the origins of man. Additionally, this therapist has worked with a number of individuals who have memories of alien abductions. This will become evident by many of the questions to follow this session.

Session II, Questions Become Interviews
August 5, 2011

Client is inducted, and contact is made after some adjustments on each end. Therapist begins questioning entity who calls himself 'Han.' He announces his presence by saying,

I am here. You may continue your questions.

Can you foresee future events?

To some extent, but not very far.

How does our planet compare to others you know of as a place for life to exist?

Although, to some extent, there are other planets like it, Earth is unique, and we enjoy it for that.

What is your home planet like?

(Steve is shown a flash of what Han's planet looks like.)

It has two suns, one farther away. On our planet there is a purpose for everyone – all interconnected spirit. There are many animals. There are oceans. We evolved from the oceans, too. We have animals that fly, live on the land, and in the oceans. As with you, salinity is part of our metabolism and other growing things, too. Our planet almost suffered extinction, but we stabilized our planet.

Is there war where you come from?

We live in harmony with each other, interconnected.

Do you have a family?

It is not a family as you think of your family, but rather a kind of longing and connection with those who come from the same place and time.

What does mathematics have to do with the Universe and creation?

Everything can be described in terms of mathematics. We still have things we do not know. What you see as chaos is just a situation where you do not know all the formulas, yet. Do not think of black holes as simply devouring holes. Think of them as 'wombs' in which life, in its elemental form, is being created. They provide a center to create and sustain every galaxy. Technology is a tool we take with us as we travel through time and space. You could describe your Universe as a mathematical model, but there is much more. Math is a universal language everywhere.

What can you tell us about crop circles?

Most of them are *not* of our making. We enjoy using the English countryside. We are often imitated. Our purpose is to show humans that they are not alone in the Universe. It is not the complex symbols, but the statement itself that is our meaning. Crop circles are the maze 'maize' of the mind (a little humor). We love to dazzle you with symmetry and to say hello.

What is on the reverse side of the moon?

It is like two moons. The other side is more topographically complex. We park there. We can pass through solid objects and go underground so you cannot see our ships there unless we want you to see them.

Can you expand on your answer concerning dark matter, which I asked about in a previous session?

It is a placeholder for the planets.

What medium carries thought?

It is an energy that we can see, but you cannot. You need to understand how you touch your environment, even with thought. Processes for thought work much faster than you can imagine.

Is time a moot point when considering the 'big bang?' What caused the big bang?

Time did not disappear at the point of the big bang. It continues to exist always, including in the other universes. The big bang occurred because the membranes of two universes bumped up against each other and this caused the explosion known as the 'big bang.'

A discussion of emotions, and individuality vs. connectivity ensued:

We, as a species have evolved to minimize our emotions. We learn from humans about emotions and their usefulness in life.

In the United States, individualism is admired and helps to promote creativity. How do you view the concept of individualism?

We see your need for individualization as being tied to fear of death, the human ego, and your inability to have real trust that allows interdependent living. Our species does not have the same kind of ego.

However, we often feel the need for individuality to some (lesser) degree. In order for us to communicate, humans must raise the bar and our species must temporarily lower the bar. The human species is an anomaly. Interaction with humans is worth our time as we continue careful interaction between us. We adapt to nature instead of changing it. It is our ecology of space for other life forms.

Session III, Spirituality, Serpo Project
August 14, 2011

The client, Steve, is placed in a deep trance and Han is invited to speak with us.

Steve: He feels like a wave of energy, like a breeze that came into a room. I feel it through my body.

I am here.

Our first question, 'How do you feel your spirituality?'

Spirituality is an acknowledgement of something beyond us that is beneficial for well-being. In a community of beings there are others in the same meditative focus. It is strange to describe. (When we look at) humans, compared to entities like us, we feel our consciousness has a sense of peace and higher purpose. The feeling we have is extended telepathically between us and it provides a sense of great spiritual being and meaningfulness. (It is) a belonging with each other and the higher being (with whom) we are in contact. It is this way with us. Our ability to communicate with each other telepathically enhances the experience.

As you know, Steve mentioned you came in like a wave of energy. A being from the Pleiades describes how they see human beings, that is, they view us as waves of energy instead of particles of energy. Is that how you see us?

It is both material and immaterial, particle and wave. The wave is the most beautiful expression for the radiated energy that ties us together, radiating from all human beings. It is not so much a material thing as ethereal form. It is like a song, a song for each, in harmony with all that makes life bearable and beautiful. It is a beautiful thing. This is what happens.

Han, I invite you to share with us the relationship that your species has with animals.

We are a form of animal, as are all living things. It is not the context that humans often place on the word 'animal.' We are a higher being much beyond our material self in a spiritual and intellectual level that has advanced. We have joined into the community of sentient beings and (it is) a delightful place.

Steve: We are holding onto my focus. He, ah, he feels reluctant to share further on that question only, but welcomes further questions.

The next question involves exchanges of human beings with other cultures not on this Earth. One program was called the Serpo Project. Are there what we might call, cultural exchanges, literal physical cultural exchanges between this planet and other planets?

There are cultures who wish to expedite contact. Some have a sense of urgency, others not so much. That contact occurred many years ago. It was partially successful. Some humans and entities did not survive the exchange. It saddened us that it was not as successful as we had hoped. It was with the best of intentions, but permanently changing residences planet-to-planet caused great emotional shock. Many of the psychological and emotional connections with other humans were severed. This was not intentional, but a sense of longing for home made for difficult transitions for many of the passengers to Serpo. Though they were well treated, there were limitations in the success of this experiment. The detachment from your planet was too great to bear. It provided a sense of adventure and exploration, but without the ability to return that knowledge, the one-way trip was an emotional strain on the occupants. The same was true for our beings during the exchange. They survived better because they were accustomed to other worlds. It was too sudden a change for humans.

The exchange of cultures and contact was premature, but we have adapted to that. Now we make contact for shorter time periods so humans can be brought back after many hours, instead of forever. The connections with family in human society are too great to sever so suddenly. In addition, they could not emotionally adapt to our culture and our ways. They were well treated and regarded with respect, but like a vine, they lived for a time and then withered and died. They could not sustain themselves. We regret that.

The policy now in effect is for short-term contact on a slow and gradual basis, with this planet and others. Yes, Serpo did exist in (making) contact in the desert of northern New Mexico. An exchange was made between both sides, in secret, and our knowledge is heightened by this. We learned a lot about human weaknesses as well as strengths as they also learned about ours. There is still a great gap in future exchanges on a long-term basis. Humans need to adapt. We have adapted, but we are accustomed to this. It was just too new an experience the first time. A new means or methods are now in place for this.

We understand different types of entities have, on occasion, either crashed here or debarked here and that some were held captive. Can you tell me how long the longest survival time was for these beings?

We observed a life signal, in the sense of a live spirit, for several years. It, too, withered like a vine. We could have interceded at any time and brought them back, but it was necessary to understand all we could. To initiate contact, the crash was staged. It was partly an intentionally staged event. This was done to watch the reactions of humans and to learn all we could. The entities who died were prepared to accept that consequence. It was sad that it had to be this way. We are more careful in preventing cultural contamination that might affect your species. Contact is now more controlled. The exchange of entities and humans was a later experiment (Serpo) that also was only partially successful.

An evolution of change was made to adapt to the situation. (This was) to make access to you possible. We were interested in your nuclear energy and its possible uses in your society. We recognized its great benefits and pitfalls, and we wished to help in monitoring and perhaps preventing mistakes that we made millions of years earlier. It, the crash, that occurred, is not common. We take care to prevent such events, but we are also mortal and, as such, we are vulnerable to mortal tendencies. It was an unfortunate 'accident' and one of several in an ongoing exploration of your world.

As you may be aware, I have been working with individuals who believe that they have made contact, usually, against their will. My primary concern is their emotional and psychological resilience and well-being. Would you care to offer some advice that I may use to help them understand and cope with the trauma?

Many of these contacts are made by beings who are performing unethical procedures that we do not condone. Part of our presence here is to monitor the activities of these other beings who often, for both selfish and unselfish reasons, exploit human physical qualities. Many of them (abductors) do not care (about) humans because of their own selfish needs. They often traumatize. Much energy is wasted in calming abductees. The context of these contacts is often not appropriate.

Is there any way for these people to resist?

There is little that they can do. They are at a great disadvantage. Usually, they are traumatized by the shock of what is occurring. It is unfortunate this is happening. It may be part of the process that will eventually become easier, with more contacts. However, they can resist by their *strength of will* and by overcoming their fear. The fear confuses and clouds perceptions and communication. *Strength of will* is the key.

If I can give suggestions to their unconscious minds to suspend their fear during these events, would that enable them to come through the events in better psychological and emotional condition?

No. Replacing fear alone will not accomplish this. Combine a suggestion to replace fear with a:

a) sense of self-worth
b) sense of being a powerful spiritual being
c) suggestion of having strength to resist in an emotional and physical sense.

The entities will be confounded by finding their subject is not so off guard. This will make it more difficult for them to carry out their purposes on unwilling subjects. Spiritual and emotional strength is the step forward.

Only suspending the fear will create a passive being. Combining the suspension of fear with self-worth and spiritual strength will make it easier for the positive energy to flow. This wave of positive energy will help create a sense of strength and help with coping with the loss of control they all experience. Control is an illusion. The experience can be accepted, but, in the end, it is their sense of self-worth that will help them prevail.

Would it be helpful to point out to these people that they are truly spiritual beings and that aspect of them cannot be harmed?

The spiritual part is on a plane that has a strength of its own that will see one through these difficult times. It is what connects to a higher being that makes such invulnerability possible.

Are these particular entities who are abducting humans actually creating a hybrid species?

Yes. Not always successfully. Their hybrids require higher maintenance and they do not always sustain themselves. They have to continually renew certain biological functions to make this happen. They are not autonomous, yet. They are trying to evolve to adapt to be more compatible in this place.

This place being Earth?

Yes.

Where are they kept while waiting to adapt? Are they kept off-planet?

Yes. Some are left for periods of time to help them socially adapt, but only for a limited period of time. The process is still ongoing, and it is difficult for them to be successful. We are also involved in seeing that, to some extent, they are not successful. We are interceding and trying to prevent further adaptation.

These hybrids are not able to procreate?

No. Not the same way. They must be produced and manufactured and the process is complex and not efficient.

I would think it would be difficult to have the resources on hand to feed them.

Certain physical needs must be met. This, too, creates a burden. Many entities can live on energy or forms of resources that are very efficient. Hybrids live as if being connected to species on Earth. They also adopt the inefficiencies of beings of this whole planet. They require certain things. They are not fully capable for living independently herc, yet.

Has what we would call a 'grey,' ever been autopsied on this planet?

Yes. Early on, in the events in New Mexico, an opportunity existed for that, but other human hoaxes have clouded a clear picture of the situation.

Is there something that you would simply like to share with us without my asking the questions?

This is an ongoing communication. We welcome this. In time, a larger picture will form about the purposes of all entities involved on all sides. Much hysteria in your culture is prevalent, surrounding our contacts with you. Some of it is fabricated and some of it is real. Some is done for their purposes, sometimes for selfish purposes. There is short-term use without understanding long-term consequences. Such is the state at this time. It will take further steps to clarify the true purpose. Part of this is the human limitation of communication with and between individuals of your species. They are vulnerable to deception and views that create strain and strife in human cultures.

Thank you for that. I think it is time to bring Steve back to this level of consciousness.

We look forward to talking to you again. Thank you. Maybe I will eventually understand why mankind is so terrified of facing something new.

We wish, with compassion, to express that many entities do not follow ethical precepts that have created this situation for your clients. (*This is a reference to the traumatized experiencers whom I regress and assist.*) We regret that, and, in our own way, we are interceding to prevent such trauma to 26 people.

Session ended.

Session IV, Others Join In, Other Dimensions
August 20, 2011

Client was in placed in a deep trance. The being known as 'Han' was requested to step forward. An invitation was extended to Han to bring someone else with him.

Steve perceived two beings coming forward with one holding to the background.

Steve: There are two! I recognize Han's shape. There is another one, in the background, standing to the side and behind him. He is similar looking.

I will address the questions to the being known as Han. When you are ready please let us know. Take your time.

(Double beeping sound.)

I'm ready.

Thank you. Thank you for bringing someone else with you.

Steve: The other one, he is the same, but also different. He is like Han in appearance, but different. I am told to 'stand by.' They have soft features, both of them. There is a kind of dark silhouette against an amber background. Han is sitting there, waiting patiently, waiting for his time to talk. He is ready for the questions.

Thank you. I will now address Han with the question.

Han, does a burst of gamma rays indicate photons coming from a fourth dimension?

Repeat the question.

Yes. Does a burst of gamma rays indicate photons coming from a fourth dimension?

The gamma rays come from a pulsar and travel through space. There will be gamma ray bursts. A gamma ray burst does travel across time, if that is what you mean by a fourth dimension. It radiates out in a burst, randomly. The gamma ray bursts are dangerous. They need to be avoided. They do indicate a distortion in time and create a bend in space that occurs naturally. These are effects of a gamma ray burst on a sun that is in a different time in life (different life stage) than the natural span of this star, which Earth people call Sol.

Thank you. Are there an infinite number of dimensions?

There are more than we possibly realize, but infinite is an ambiguous term. It might be true, but there are more than humans realize, and there may be more than even we realize.

With how many dimensions does your species interact?

Steve: My mind from Han says '26 dimensions at present.' It is astonishing!

The next question has to do with the beginning of our Universe. Did some particles move into the fourth dimension during the beginning of our Universe?

These particles are dark matter that permeated the membrane between Universes. These are the particles to which you refer. Yes. The particles can permeate universes and provide us with the means to travel across the vast distances. We can step across one universe for a shortcut that provides us a brief distance in which to travel wherever we wish to go. When we step back into the former universe, the dark matter helps provide the river in which we flow between universes to make this possible, to use a simple analogy.

Thank you. How might we human beings detect the fourth dimension?

The fourth dimension is around us. My mind sees a parallax view where a simple observation could make this possible, but it is difficult to discern how this is possible. However, scientists can learn by using two vantage points in parallax view to see a simple shift in matter across space where, for example, a pulsar might find a type of shift that could allow the fourth dimension to be evident in its existence.

Thank you. Concerning dark energy, two questions:

1) *What is its chemical composition?*
2) *Does it push the material world apart?*

It co-exists in the existing material world. It actually makes up the majority of the material world, the material universe. It is not evident unless one looks across the vastness of space where most of it can be seen in quantity. It provides the balance of what composes the Universe. The existence of dark energy requires more advanced concepts regarding energy, mass, and gravity and how they are brought into harmony. This 'bringing together' creates the complete perspective of the composition of the Universe. It is what Earth scientists wish to find in a unified theory that will make everything under-standable. However, this understanding will only be the beginning of further understanding. Once this unified theory is understood, it will provide a doorway for many things, as it did for us, millions of years ago, to facilitate uses of energy on a planetary scale and to provide the means of transportation between stars.

There is a current theory that dark energy is what is causing the Universe to kind of spread out. Is that an accurate view?

The Universe is expanding from its beginning source. It accelerates the expansion of all that exists in this Universe. The existence of dark matter is what makes this expansion and acceleration possible. It is what puzzles scientists on Earth, the condition where there is no entropy, but just acceleration of matter as it expands outward.

If I understand, are you saying the characteristic of expansion is such that, over time and space, it increases its velocity?

Yes, it does.

Thank you. I have a question about dark matter. We (humans) have been using a dedicated telescope to try to map a general picture of the Universe and the map that we have come up with looks rather like a neural network with long interconnecting filaments between solar systems and galaxies. It is the current belief that dark matter is what allows this to happen -- that it provides a kind of base for attracting stars, galaxies, and larger systems. The overall picture seems to be one of interconnectiveness. Would you comment on that?

There are many nurseries for stars where many stars are created in the same nebulous clouds. These naturally form together as the masses in these nebulous (clouds) contract, become denser, and then create nuclear fusion to ignite as stars. These nurseries naturally form in clusters as the Universe, itself, through dark matter, continues to expand and accelerate, spreading outward, like an explosion. Where the dust and the matter of space condense, it changes in mid-explosion.

If one could imagine in the analogy of an explosion in several seconds compared with the expansion of the Universe in billions of years, stars are born, change, evolve, die, and create more matter. This, in turn, produces the matter from which all building blocks of the Universe exist, including the building blocks of life.

The positions of these stars are naturally created from broad areas of nebulous clouds. That is often the explanation for the accumulation of stars. There are areas of space that are rather devoid of stars. This is rare, and, in time, this will permeate everywhere. This mass comes from the original focus point where the dark matter entered from the other universe and gave birth to this Universe. It is a natural process. The Universe in this dimension will seem to be infinite, but it is still expanding, and what is beyond is still unknown, even to us.

Is there some kind of a connection within a solar system or galaxy, some kind of energy connection of what we might term 'lay lines' for instance, between our planets, other than the connection of gravity?

There is the gravity that connects the stars and the planets and ultimately the galaxies. There is also a connection of dark matter that is less conspicuous in binding and connecting together. It is like a form of gelatin or gelatin-like material around a galaxy and *the dark matter is this gelatin.* It holds in place the more conspicuous parts of matter, binding and holding it together and moving together. Everything is moving. This dark matter holds the parts of the Universe we see together in a loose fluid, much like a cloud, an invisible cloud that pulls the galaxy together. At the other end, in the center of the galaxy, is often a black hole that acts as an anchor around which all other objects orbit. This creates a suspension matter or dark matter around the circumference of the galaxy. The dark center creates the vehicle for which gravity and matter can move in a uniform pattern.

Thank you. I heard a comment on the radio that there is either a comet or an asteroid headed toward Earth and behind it is a planet that may have been caught up in our original orbit. Do you know something about a rather long-term journey of a planet that is actually coming in behind one of these objects that may affect life as we know it on Earth?

No. There is a comet approaching within 90 million miles. It will pass harmlessly, though close. It is not a concern for us and for this Earth planet.

Session ended.

Session V, Universe and Human Evolution
August 28, 2011

The first four sessions were prepared without categorization. Starting with Session V, categories were introduced to group information. These categories are:

Earth History
Zeta Reticuli History
Spirituality
Contact
The Universe
Other
Open Session for Comments or Questions

(Not all categories are used in each session.)

Steve was inducted, given some therapy and then the being known as Han was invited to step forward. After several adjustments, Han identified himself by saying,

I am ready.

Steve: He is alone this time. I feel a smile from him, not a physical one, but a thought, expressing a smile and his readiness. I feel a shudder through my body as if I am being released. I didn't anticipate that.

Earth History

Are we human beings a kind of genetic alphabet soup with lots of junk DNA?

Do you have junk DNA? If that is so, then we also have junk DNA for we are not genetically dissimilar from each another in many ways. Part of the amalgamation of evolution and adaptation is a normal process. Any junk DNA is the foundation on which we have achieved this point in time where we are genetically at this moment. Certain key genes often get more attention than others do as evolution develops, as we continue to strive forward. It is the same for both your species and ours. This is a natural process. No gene is debased. It is just not being utilized at the moment. Just like the genes for hands are active, other parts remain passive for the moment, while other parts develop. Does that answer your question?

Yes. I had thought perhaps that such a variety of unused DNA also provides potential for quick adaptations in the event of an environmental change.

Just as your species often stores body fat as a survival function, so does a surplus of DNA exist for adaptation as needed. You may view them as spare parts for adjusting to future conditions. In a way, no DNA is wasted or is junk. It is just in reserve, as building blocks stored away if needed at the appropriate time for the evolutionary process. It makes a species successful, along with its intellect, to adapt to new conditions. The intellect is fleeting, but evolution is a broader process that stands over a greater length of space and time in which it manifests itself. You are a vulnerable species, prone to external influences and adaptations. *That is partially why we are here to protect you from outside influences that may have other plans that are more selfish and not helpful to your species.*

Your emotional state is more pronounced than in our species. In a way, it should be better controlled within yourselves. At the same time, you have a positive side to your emotions. You have that emotional drive and passion for exploration, which we lack. We do share curiosity, however. The negative emotions can prevail, too, and it creates turmoil between the positive and the negative. This windstorm of emotions within you can sometimes create either a coherence or incoherence in your society in how you approach problems and take care of your emotional well-being. This creates confusion. We are so often in contact with you. Often, you are not as calm when we are trying to communicate with you. Your species needs to calm down, relax, and clear your minds to be more receptive to our communication. This will take time. We are patient.

What is the missing link for humans? One theory is that we descended from a combination of the Neanderthal man and Homo sapiens. Have we had more than one branch of humanity, and, if not, do you know what species is the missing link?

The evolution of man is a varied one. However, it is not as complex as man makes it to be. There are many idiosyncrasies in the evolution of Homo sapiens. We have often nurtured, guided, and influenced to mold a species that is more receptive to eventually make contact with us and with others in the Universe. This takes time. Many links exist. It is just that all the links in the chain have not yet been discovered by you, but in time, perhaps they will.

How many branches gave rise to the human species?

The best we can tell is that there were six branches. Some were not successful. Others endured longer and two or three have merged into one main species forming the current Homo sapiens that we know today.

How would you compare the intelligence of dolphins, whales, and rats to human beings, with intelligence defined as the capacity to learn?

Whales and dolphins have larger brains and therefore the capacity for growth. They have an intellectual capacity near that of human beings. They lack the ability to create technology because they have not adapted to move upon the land where they can create fire and change the minerals of the natural world into alloys to create technology. Technology is not important to intellect, but it is a useful tool for expressing intellect as man has done. The rat has very instinctual primitive impulses in how it survives. Whales and dolphins are beyond that in being creative and in adapting to their environment. They are more at one with their environment. Our species, the way we react, and our quick thinking, are more similar to your species of birds. We are sharp-witted and react quickly, but our intellect has a much greater capacity than your birds. However, the reactions of birds are very similar to our species in the thought processes that exist. Whales and dolphins are similar to man in potential for thought capacity, but they lack the ability to leave the ocean to move into an environment where there is air and oxygen in which to create fire. From fire they can create further conditions of benefit to them.

Are you familiar with the Nazca lines? If so, what is their source and purpose?

Yes. It is an expression of connection with the sky and those beings who have come from the sky to visit. It is like a welcome mat for home. It is an expression by your species of gratitude and appreciation and welcome in the hope that further contact will be made. It is a physical expression of a desire within man's heart to make contact with all that is above him in the sky.

Did humans make these after becoming aware of beings in the sky? Was it expressing a desire to have them return?

Yes. It is an expression of welcome in the hope they will return. We do return, but sometimes in other forms. Each return is appropriate to the era of man's development. The form and means of contact has now changed to a more sophisticated and perhaps on a more individual level with your species.

Was the story of Atlantis real? If so, where is it? What caused its demise?

There is an area off of what was once near Ireland in the ocean. That island has since sunk below the ocean. It was isolated from the nearby cultures where we could educate humans with more advanced ideas and abilities than the other areas of your planet. This culture enjoyed many of the benefits of our knowledge and technologies. This was a test to see what you could do with this new technology, if used for good purposes, which it was. It gave us encouragement to use this as a basis for sharing other technology in the future. The demise of this large island was due to the geology of your planet. Eventually the humans migrated off that island into Europe and the Mediterranean. They had to do this in order to survive. This knowledge was dispersed among the cultures in the area. Over time, much of this knowledge was lost due to the poor means available to preserve such knowledge.

Much of what was to be passed on from generation to generation was eventually lost because of the subjectivity of the human mind. It was not passed on efficiently. Also, many cultures on Earth destroyed this knowledge. Some of it was lost due to mishandling or carelessness in preserving this knowledge. It is just part of the human condition. This is so. We needed to create a way for them to preserve this knowledge in an intact way. However, it would have been inappropriate to give them the technology to do this. It would be like giving a computer to primitive form of your society in order to hold this knowledge. Many ancient libraries were lost due to fire, such as in Alexandria. In other cultures, a more dogmatic culture prevailed. All this needs to be restored.

Did any of this knowledge wind up in what we call the Mystery Schools?

Certain isolated pockets in Europe held onto knowledge, but it was quickly distorted by outsiders and misinterpreted as something evil or not beneficial. It was due to certain biases in belief that this knowledge waned and was lost over time. In purges of new political and social mores, it was – the knowledge, in a sense, was scattered to the wind. Man did not possess the ability to preserve this knowledge, particularly in an unbiased way. However, the test was successful for a brief time. It was a temporary condition on Atlantis, so an island country did exist.

What did they call their island?

I don't remember.

How many times has mankind risen and fallen in terms of advanced technology?

Man, in isolated pockets around the world, has advanced greatly, and like water, this advancement ebbs and flows with the times. In the Middle East there was great advancement in mathematics and societies. Then, in time, this was lost due to selfishness and wars as other societies dominated them with less knowledge. Usually, they incorporated the knowledge of the conquering societies. This has been an ongoing condition within the limited viewpoints and the geographical inability to travel over great distances. Isolated pockets of knowledge come and go. This is less so now. You now have the ability to communicate across greater distances within your species. You have also learned to preserve it. Due to this, no one particular idea will dominate.

Would it be reasonable to say that pockets of advancement have occurred many times in small areas?

Yes. It is an evolution where some have advanced forward. There are also short-term setbacks, then more advances, then more setbacks. Human advancement is limited only by the ability of technology to communicate across the Earth, along with the ability to travel. In time, the information becomes more prevalent and more diverse where more people can compare and experience other ideas more freely.

What can you tell us about big foot, sasquatch, or yeti?

On your planet, there are many species yet to be discovered. These are predominantly in the oceans of your world. There are areas of land that are still quite isolated and there are offshoots, or as you call them, missing links. They have the ability to conceal themselves and live secretly in peace away from the dominating influence of the human species that tends to propagate across the surface of your planet. There are isolated pockets where life exists and these life forms conceal themselves so that any evidence of their existence is difficult to find. Such are the creatures that you call yeti and big 'feet.' *(The therapist smiled over this failure to understanding that it is big foot.)* There is speculation that they are an offshoot of an alien species, but they are, in fact, indigenous to this planet. We have often encountered them and have contacted them along with many other species here, and we understand the delicate relationship, a precarious one that exists between their species and the human species. We try not to interfere so that one does not become aware of the other, in fear that the yeti species will be overrun and become extinct.

Do they bury their dead?

They know fire and they extinguish their bodies in such a manner so that very little remains. This is done to help conceal any remnants of them. Others withdraw into caves where they live. Mostly, they will die there in the darkest recesses of the Earth so that the remains are not discovered. They do this with an overwhelming devotion to their species because they know that human beings would dominate and destroy their culture. It is not so much fear of humans as it is a love for their own species, as precarious as they are. They live in isolation, one with nature, and the planet. It is a shame that human species cannot adapt and learn from them. I fear that they would be overwhelmed and swallowed up and become extinct. Their toehold on the planet is one that is the natural process of your planet. They are a noble species and one that is at one with the planet. They live as part of it. The planet is their mother. They love their mother and their mother loves them. It is an analogy. This is something Native Americans also knew and other cultures around the planet, but as technology over-whelms cultures, these teachings are lost in time. The Big Foot could be a teacher for human society, but I am afraid that will not happen in time.

Yes. I hope specimens have been taken and they flourish on other planets, too.

You have anticipated what we have already done. The individual cultures may be gone, but someday it is possible they will be reintroduced. They exist on other worlds now, preserved. If appropriate, they could be brought back to this world. Like many species I spoke of earlier that are transplanted on other worlds, some of those other worlds can transplant things here. The Yeti can be one of those.

It gives me lots of hope.

All is not lost. It is a vast universe with infinite possibilities and hope. The Earth is a test tube. Surrounding it is the greater laboratory, with many other specimens preserved for the future.

Zeta Reticuli History

Questions were deferred to later sessions.

Spirituality

Is having a soul, spirit, or consciousness a preexisting condition for all material life forms?

An energy exists that transcends all.

It is part of that same released soul energy that is passed on to future bodies when the physical body dies.

This energy is connected to a part of what makes life in the Universe. There are still aspects of this that we do not understand, but we know it exists. We can take this knowledge with us. We take solace in knowing that there are energies and dimensions of the Universe where this energy co-mingles with life in a physical sense and also extends beyond, in a spiritual sense. I hope I can explain so you can under-stand. It is a mystery to us, too.

Can souls transfer to other species?

This occurs only where the species has the same or greater intellect. To pass a soul on to a plant would be a waste. We, our souls, are often passed on to species that can live comfortably within the confines of a physical body and that can be across the Universe.

In the case of a clone, does it have a soul?

The clone is a physical copy of a known physical prototype. The clone should have a soul, because cloning is just a different form of duplicating life. Where there is life, there is the possibility of life energy or soul.

Perhaps they share the same soul as the original.

That is uncertain, but it is an interesting question.

What can you tell us about the large black cube at Mecca, including the black rock embedded in it? It is a place of worship for Muslims.

I do not know of this cube. I do know that their religious faith is focused on this location. However, the belief in their god should not be limited to just a location.

Contact

How would you describe the gelatin-like substance found in tubes that abductees describe breathing during abductions?

I do not understand the context.

Humans report being abducted, taken onto ships, and placed in tubes that were filled with a material that they had to breathe in. They were able to do this, but it was a substance with a consistency of jelly. It also seemed to provide some kind of cushioning for the human body.

We have mentioned hybridization. Know that this is part of the hybridization program of another species. We work to limit the species that is trying to adapt themselves to life on this planet (Earth). It is not a human process, but a hybrid process. It is a form of a nursery for growing hybrids that are both human and alien. The humans observed in this condition are not completely human.

Are there hybrids living among humans that go undetected?

Yes. For limited periods. Their ability to function in human society is limited. It takes a process to extend their lives. It is far from being complete.

Using remote viewing, can Steve touch an alien, another species from another planet? In other words, can he have a tactile experience?

Reality in the mind is many things. In a physical sense, perhaps it is not. In a remote viewing sense it is possible. For the human mind and the alien mind reality is only what each perceives it to be. The human has the desire to touch. It is part of its makeup and makes it special. It is part of what gives an emotional sense of well-being. We, too, can understand this, but it is not often in physical touch. However, this can be the case. We can understand that, so in a physical sense, at the moment, unless physical contact is made, it would be impossible. However, through the connection between minds, with enough feeling, touch is possible.

You are saying that Steve could enjoy the experience?

Yes. He is not far from that already.

Did an alien presence intrude into a secured nuclear weapons area at the Royal Air Force Base at Woodbridge/Bentwaters in December 1980? If so, why?

The human understanding of that event is correct. These intrusions are to monitor the existence and potential use of dangerous weapons in storage. We monitor these sites often, along with other species. It is done for the purpose of the safety of our, shall we say, our investment in the human species so that they will not destroy themselves and at the same time, safeguard our own species. A contact at that base was made. It caused a disturbance. Occasionally, a demonstration of our existence is necessary on a scale that is equal to the task. It was important to monitor the weapons of these nations and to also test that we can still disable them, if necessary, and to monitor the current level of technology of these crude weapons in our ability to control those weapons in the future.

Thank you for monitoring. Humans are not necessarily good decision makers.

The Universe

At the beginning of this Universe, was there a fluid composed of quarks and gluon fields that had properties of both dense and less dense characteristics that enabled patterns to form?

There are basic building blocks for physical universes, called atoms, but within atoms are other building blocks that compose the atoms. Beyond that are building blocks even more simplistic which you have not yet discovered. The items that you mentioned compose part of that. In the relationship of what composes physical matter, often these understandings will help you in future to understand this better and to travel within that universe in time.

While we have not yet discovered them, are there a finite number of them?

There is a curious surprise between dark matter and what you call non-dark matter that will help link together into a unified understanding of the Universe. These elements also compose what you call anti-matter. You will understand in time that this anti-matter will help facilitate the travel I mentioned earlier. These elements compose the number of elements.

Steve: In my mind there are 52, but I don't know what it means. Han is not being forthcoming on everything. I think he wants us to be surprised.

How many planets sustain species of humans?

It depends on how you define human beings. In 'like frequencies of light' there is a bandwidth, which includes what we call humans. The humans on this planet are part of an evolution started long ago. It conceals the fact that, because of the distance in time, humans feel that they originated here, but actually, *the seed was planted in many areas of the Universe.* There are also many species that you may refer to as 'aliens.' We are actually, in a distant way, your relatives. Around the Universe, part of our seeding of other planets has made this possible. The 'aliens' that are often seen as foreign to you are ancestors and a glimpse of your future at the same time. There are many examples of human beings and you should not feel diminished by this. Rather, you should only feel magnified that you are part of a larger family, separated by a distance, which seems great to you only because of your level of development in technology. There is an interconnected family beyond, out there, about which one should feel good.

You are not alone.

Other

Not used this session.

Open Session for Comments or Questions

Please comment on anything you like or ask anything you like.

Each life form has its own reality. What is reality to one is a different reality to another. Humans have their own reality. We have our own reality. This communication merges and creates a different reality that is broadening in its scope and will make understanding better and create new perspectives of the Universe and what it means to each. In some ways, you are very confined.

Steve is very receptive for communication. He is also limited, too. However, we are, too, just in a broader sense, so we understand his efforts to facilitate and make himself available for communication with us. In a greater sense, he is a part of everything, as are you. I am pleased with the questions you asked. They help explain our motives, such as our activities at Rendalsham. Our purpose in interacting with hybrids is an expression of our wish to limit abductions on this planet. We want to take these narrow avenues of communication and to make them blossom as fully as we can, to take the opportunity to communicate our perspectives with you today.

What can I do in terms of my own beliefs to facilitate that for you?

To continue on your pathway. You are receptive and a good servant to the needs of facilitating communication between our species. To continue on the path that you have lived and continue to do so. Take the hope with you that you are creating a beneficial and positive situation.

End of session.

Chapter Two: Alien Biology and Consciousness

Session VI, Alien Biology, God
September 4, 2011

Client was inducted, and Han was invited to communicate.

I am here.

Steve: I can see him. He is tan. He is very skinny. His skin is a light brown. His neck is long and very thin. I don't see how he can hold up his head. His fingers are long and very thin. There are pads on the ends.

Earth History

Are you familiar with the name Albert Einstein? Where did his ideas come from?

Yes. His ideas are primarily his own. He had many other fine qualities that included a moral philosophy concerning human behavior. He regretted his indirect contribution to the human development of atomic weapons, but he has no reason to have felt that way. His contribution was considerable, natural, and necessary along the correct path to further human understanding of the Universe. We only regret that the normal individual human span of life is short, which denied him a more complete and unified understanding of the Universe.

Zeta Reticuli History

What can you tell me about the growing and collecting of food for your species? Do you primarily use robotics?

We use both robots and our own species to grow and gather food. We also gather food from other planets thus creating a nice variety. We have created the species that you call 'greys' to help us with our ships.

How do you ingest the food – as liquid, or both liquid and harder substances requiring chewing?

We have a liquid. We also have something of an applesauce consistency. We like the apples of your planet, and they, with adjustments, have been planted on our and other planets.

How does your species educate its young?

They do not go to schools in your sense. They are taught in an environment that you might call home schooling. They are well educated in mathematics and many other areas, as needed. This is done telepathically. There is great exposure to a very large body of knowledge from an early age.

Are there specialized studies such as research or medicine?

Yes. We still have doctors, as you call them, for we are still a mortal species and sometimes get injured or ill. Much of our need for 'doctors' has been replaced with greater immunity to illnesses, built into our genetic identity as a species.

What is birth like for your species?

It is not birth as you know it. It is a mechanical process. When one being is ready to expire, we prepare another one to takes its place. We carefully control our numbers according to the environmental availability of each planet.

What is the life expectancy?

We live a very long time.

(Answer was evasive, but was answered specifically later on.)

Steve: We have many things that make us human. Part of what makes us human is our art. If only Han could experience the theater, the symphony hall, the opera house, the movies, the museums; read poems, hear stories, see the paintings of da Vinci, Georgia O'Keefe, and Picasso; experience a Greek tragedy or a comedy by Shakespeare; hear Louis Armstrong, Mozart, and Oklahoma; see the grace of dancers, or the elegance of a bow crossing the strings of a violin; or the profundity of a child drawing a picture of her mother.

Steve: Does Han's civilization have art? Can Han describe what art is for his species?

Yes. We do have something that you would call art. We have monuments from long ago. We also enjoy music. Art is an expression of what we are as a species, a keynote of our past, present, and future.

We ask for a demonstration, using Steve's body as the receptacle for music.

We can accommodate that.

Please begin now.

Steve begins describing a feeling like drumming or pulsing, but without any definite rhythm.

Steve: I sense no sound, more emotion. There are layers of many emotions with many rhythms at the same time. There is a harmony. There are too many notes, first pulsing, then serene, then a finish. Like a symphony, it changes tempo. It is more sophisticated than a poem. It is like Beethoven's Pastoral, without sound, just emotion.

Does your species have a male and female or are you androgynous?

Yes. We retain the characteristics of male and female on the inside, but not on the outside.

Spirituality

What was the purpose and composition of the Arc of the Covenant?

It could be dangerous. It was a portal to other realties. The last place known was in a cave. I see its general geographic location. It is best I share no further on this.

Contact

Steve would like the experience of touching you (Han). Is this permissible at this time?

Yes. This can be arranged.

Steve: I am reaching out to touch his forearm now. It feels cool. It feels smooth and, at the same time, leathery. I am touching his hand. He is touching mine. He turns his hand up. I can feel a kind of overall pulsing in his hand. It does not feel like a boney, skeletal feeling, but it feels more like a kind of cartilage. It is rigid, but when I touch it gently, it seems to have certain elasticity like plastic. He is touching my hand and I can feel his mind, through his fingers, probing and gathering information.

I extend my hand up his forearm touching gently, but respectfully no farther, so as not to intrude into his space. I rest my palm on top of his to show an expression of openness and trust. I then extend my other palm underneath his supporting his hand and my other hand. I am gently holding his hand between mine. His fingers are long and spindly. I sense they have many nerve endings there. Han and I seem to be exchanging thoughts, as if we are now, strangely, directly wired. Astonished, I withdraw my hands, and Han withdraws his. This creates a brief moment of reflection, then further questions.

During abductions, or any human contact with aliens, are there any biohazards to humans from direct contact with extraterrestrials?

Yes. Often, contact between other beings and humans are through contact with species you commonly call greys. These beings are constructed in a manner that makes them biologically neutral. Full biological entities use invisible fields to protect all concerned from any potential harmful effects.

The Universe

What is the particle or element that allows other particles to have mass? Is this theory even useful (Boson particle) AKA the God particle?

The Boson particle. That is just the beginning of your knowledge and is insufficient to explain mass.

Does true randomness exist in the Universe?

It depends upon one's vantage point. At the highest levels there would not be randomness or chaos.

Can local gravity be altered using an electromagnetic field?

There are frequencies of gravity across dimensions as well. An electromagnetic field would be one small wavelength of such gravity.

What can you share with us regarding tachyons (particles that are faster than the speed of light)?

The speed of light is only of interest because your species thinks in a linear manner regarding travel. We use a different mechanism that makes the speed of light no longer relevant. Tachyons are an effect, not a cause of faster-than-light physics.

Travel beyond the speed of light – does it create a kind of bubble in the space/time continuum?

Time dilation makes faster-than-light travel impractical for timely trade and relevant timely contact between species on other planets. There are means in which interdimensional travel minimizes time dilation, to make such travel practical.

Travel by linear time may be too slow, making the purpose of such a journey meaningless by the time the destination is reached.

(Excerpt from a Coast-to-Coast-A.M. speaker.) According to Nassim Haramein, a deeper fractal reality is occurring in which atoms are like little black holes, if you scale the size of the Universe down to its smallest components. 'The Universe is learning about itself – the information that it gathers, coalesces and synergizes to produce the next set of questions, in a kind of self-organizing feedback structure.'

Would you comment on these concepts?

We are just now studying this phenomenon. My congratulations to the writer of this concept. It embraces, in our understanding, a new form of scientific philosophy.

Other

Is water the vehicle for carrying telepathic messages?

Water has many interesting qualities. Many forms of life are composed of water. It is also a good conductor of thought as well as sound.

Open Session for Comments or Questions

Do you have any comments before I close this session?

These sessions are beneficial. We look forward to further contacts.

**Session VII, Interplanetary Treaties, DNA Comparison
September 11, 2011**

Steve was inducted. He begins describing what he sees during the initial induction.

Steve: I see this gray cloud in my mind and Han is sort of in the middle of it, like a fog. It's not a cloud. It is just like an image. He is there. I feel myself floating. I like the clouds. Han is holding up his hand in greeting. My hands feel really heavy and my arms, too. I am sinking into the clouds. He is just waiting. Nice to see him (Han) again. In my mind I can see you (the therapist) and I can see him, sitting in the same room with me on the couch. Nice of him to use me to communicate to you.

Han is sitting on a bench, a piano bench. He has long skinny legs that touch the floor and he is leaning over looking at me with his hands clasped in his lap. He is waiting for me, when the time is right. I have never seen all of him before. He looks very relaxed. He is leaning over from his seat and facing me. It feels like I am in your living room on the sofa there and sitting near the piano. Near the table and chair is Han. He has a large head. I get this feeling like he's a Cheshire cat. He is playful this time and is patiently waiting. His mind has so much wisdom in it. I can see him shifting his weight, putting his hand on his leg and now he is putting it back on his lap, folding his hands together. We are ready.

Earth History

Was there ever an aerial war in our distant past, maybe 2,000 years ago?

An aerial war?

Yes.

There are certain understandings, what you would call treaties between various visiting civilizations, specifying how they are to conduct themselves in contact with humans. Those that did not have the best intentions for Earth applied certain arrangements and pressures to certain civilizations. These aspirations were restrained to create a reasonably safe and neutral area of space that includes Earth and many other planets. This might be what you call aerial warfare.

That is probably it. The reference comes from very old writings in India and a description of ships in the sky, fighting.

I understand the Hindu texts. They give insights into the background of a number of civilizations that have come to Earth. These Indian texts have many clear insights and provide early information on contact with humans.

Han, can you tell me how many planets your species inhabit now?

We inhabit many hundreds over a wide area of the galaxy. Some planets are well inhabited. Others have our mark through terraforming. There are many hundreds.

We are just now beginning to discover what we call habitable planets. I suspect that some of those may be inhabited by your species.

(No response.)

Regarding bipedalism, the ability for a species to walk on two legs, the question is, ' Was that an important evolutionary step?' Do you have any comments on that?

Many life forms are bipedal. With the beginning of standing upright and the development of tools, in a way, your species is an allegory of our species. In our evolution, we originated from a varied life form that might be considered more bird-like. We were creatures with multiple origins, not uniquely bird-like, but with some bird-like characteristics. These bird-like characteristics faded, and we became more the humanoid creature that you see presently before you. Part of our evolution was to stand upright, as your evolution from primates directed you to stand upright.

So the usefulness of bipedalism was primarily to enable the creation of tools?

Actualizing the forehands or forelegs to become arms and hands enables the creation tools. These developments are part of the process for the development of technology. Many humanoids developed these characteristics on their own. The person you know as Darwin, with his theory of natural selection, identified the pattern for the development of advanced species. In the process of intelligent selection, this created the basis from which your civilization and our civilization developed independently over time.

Concerning the human species and our brain, I understand that we only use about 10 per cent of our brain. I don't know if that is accurate, or it is simply that the other part of our brain is used in ways that we don't understand. Do you have any knowledge about that?

The human brain is still evolving and developing. It has great potential. There are very short life spans for many life forms on your planet. That creates a more rapid process of development and adaptation. As your species evolves, your minds are also of interest because we can see the potential that you perhaps do not yet grasp. Our ability to communicate telepathically is a latent ability that you do not yet know you possess. It can usually only be activated in our presence (or among other telepathic beings). That is why many humans are astonished that they can communicate telepathically with us. However, between humans, you are generally unable to do so. The potential for such communication is already there, but humans do not yet understand their abilities. Telepathy between us and other advanced species is the link that joins thoughts across the Universe. What results is, on a very basic level, an accord of attitudes. Additionally, there is a concurrence of consciousness.

Concerning our DNA, do we have any DNA in common with your species?

DNA is a combination of a number of compounds in the right combination. Much of our DNA has similar pattern arrangements as your species does. We are not too dissimilar, and there may be some long past origin between our species. The human combination is unique and extraordinary.

There is a question about what the human species might look like in 10,000 years. Just projecting out, can you see some physical adaptations that might take place over roughly 10,000 years, if you assume that the current rate of change is constant?

Ten thousand years in Earth time is a not too distant future to project. Humans would probably be taller or smaller, depending on the availability of food sources and their diet. There will probably be less body hair and larger heads. Their bodies will become slimmer.

In the development of space travel, this will begin to accelerate many changes in the human species as evolution begins to adapt the human body to a weightless environment. Right now, it has challenges adapting because technology moves faster than evolution can accommodate. In time, bodies will become taller, slimmer, more delicate, and not too dissimilar from our appearance, which was also affected by space travel.

Zeta Reticuli History

Steve would like you to describe, as much as you would like, your planet. You did describe it to some extent. He would be interested in such things as: what materials were used for your buildings; what are some of the day-to-day social activities, or whatever you would like to share.

We often miss images of home. We often have memories. We have telepathic links at home to project 'form' memories of where our life began. We often have what you might call 'homesickness.' Notwithstanding, our species has matured sufficiently to have a sophisticated understanding of life. As a result, we know that home is where you make it. We also consider Earth our home to a limited degree. It is not so much an occupied space. It is just the location.

On our home planet we see orange skies, warm sunsets, lush green hills with much food, and many peaceful landscapes. There is a serenity to home. Many places on Earth remind us of home. This question prompts not only memories, but also longings for our past home. We have oceans. I remember stating they have full, abundant life. Our cities are underground, close to the air, canyons, and valleys. They provide a metropolis for much happiness, intellectual pursuit, and a sense of well-being that comes from interconnectivity. The societies of our cities are not so much composed of physical bodies, but the proximity of many minds, which are able to interact in an orderly, coherent way, without the din of many thoughts flooding in. We can be selective and enjoy each in his own way. I miss the richness of the proximity of many minds. What you refer to as a large metropolis city, is, for us, a metropolis of telepathic minds sharing our 'connectiveness'. It is enriching. It provides security and enjoyment that comes from many of our species congregating together. That is all I wish to say about my home now.

The emotion of 'homesickness,' yes, I know it, too. A rather curious emotion and I wonder why it is part of us. What purpose does it serve? I am thinking it is part of the evolutionary process and probably had an original purpose.

In the span of time, there is a beginning and an ending. Homesickness is a symptom of the fondness of the beginning. One views their originating home with fondness and affection. On a fundamental level, the mind then explores realities beyond. From this grows the courage to explore new realities, both on a personal level, and on a species' level. A species explores the outer parts of the Universe beyond their own originating point. Our species are explorers.

At the beginning time for your species, I am guessing that you did not come from primates, but perhaps from a somewhat different creature. Is that the case?

We developed from a creature that is similar on other planets, but is unique on ours. This creature had some bird-like features and some features that were not bird-like. In combination, this creature was the forbearer of our current species. It was an entirely different creature with which humans are unfamiliar. It had many bird-like features, which would be the closest to your creatures on Earth. They have many other features, too. They did not have feathers. In much the way birds developed from dinosaurs, so our species developed from a bird-like hybrid creature.

Do you know what the skin texture was like?

The closest on your planet would be an amalgamation of many features from several species. It had a humanoid crouching body, but with some bird-like bone structure and a large head. There was no beak, the way you regard a beak.

Would you affix that picture in Steve's mind so he can visualize it?

The skin is grayer. It was a kind of neutral skin color, similar to a bat. It had an ability to fly, but has since lost that. It became more a land animal. The head developed and became so large that, in the evolutionary process, it made flying impossible. The bodies were no longer capable of flying, but there was a rapid development in intelligence. Over time, the creature lost its wings, and evolution changed it to a being that instead had long arms with hands that were originally part of a wing structure. This changed to become, more or less, the being you see today. Compared to humans, we have a rather slim body with long arms and legs with extra joints in the legs.

During that process of evolution for your species, was there ever an intervention from off-planet beings who perhaps changed your genetic codes?

Yes. We feel that there was a hybridization that accelerated our evolutionary process and more clearly defined us.

Were they from the same star system, Zeta Reticuli?

No. They were farther beyond, another advanced, migrating species that explored, as we do today. They became the greys that we think of as a full life form. They interacted with our species and we became very similar to greys, but taller. Later, they became a kind of a generic prototype form, which is used in many worlds. It has formed a model for biotechnological beings. Now, many that appear as greys are not greys, but biosynthetic forms of artificial intelligence. They have what you call technology within them. They now form a large bulk of our society and the society on other planets. They are used for many tasks, such as collecting food and exploration. They conduct many of the menial tasks and make many high-risk explorations. Initial contacts with other worlds are often through these biosynthesized beings that are not full life forms.

I can see the practicality of using them.

They can still represent our societies and our agendas. In our exploration, they can conduct our missions for us. Later, supplemental explorations by fully developed life forms often follow. When our species work toward the development of newly explored areas, they follow closely behind these pathfinders.

Does your species require sleep?

Yes. We require sleep. It is often not a physical sleep, but a mind sleep, much the way the whale might sleep. We are partially functioning, yet still conscious. Part of our minds will be resting and a portion of our minds will always be active. The human mind often has a similar division of work and rest, voluntary and involuntary activity in the human mind. We can work and rest at the same time to a degree.

When you are in this state, do you dream?

We understand the subconscious mind in humans. We often use the subconscious mind of humans when we interact with them. The subconscious mind dreams when we rest. We understand dreams, too. We have dreams that are quite clear and profound. Our type of sleep is different from human sleep, as are our dreams. Sometimes our dreams can become another form of reality. Our minds can float between two places at once.

Spirituality

Do you or are you able to communicate with the spirits of your ancestors?

Our minds can make contact on different dimensions, sometimes with the ancestors of our past, as you call it. That energy or the faint imprint of a life form will remain after the physical body is gone. This is a part of our interconnectivity. Not only can we connect with others of our species in the present time, but we can, with special training, develop the ability to go into the past to connect with the energies and life forces of past lives. The energy that life forms have from the past lingers on. What you might call ghosts today are actually just our species' thoughts and energies of past life forms. With special training, we can often touch and connect with these. It is an extension of our telepathic ability to do this.

What do the characteristics of the spirit world mean to your species?

Our species is like an interconnective weave. There are places where life forms have expired, but the imprint on the fabric of space and time exists and continues. These form a kind of spiritual heritage from our past lives, connecting with our current lives. These abilities exist in humans, too, but they are not as accessible at the current level of human evolution. They do not fully appreciate this ability, yet. In time they will.

Our species seems to have more connection with its spiritual past lives. The wisdom of the past can be passed on to the current generation, on many different wavelengths. Wherein with human abilities, they require history to be recorded for it to be passed on. In our species, history is passed on through thoughts, energies, motivations, and intentions. Our past has a much clearer understanding and interpretation in applying its history to the present time. Spiritual connections are part of a larger picture related to past lives with present lives.

There is a belief system that people are reincarnated and sometimes they remember their past lives. Does that seem like a valid explanation to you?

In our spiritual beliefs, we feel that what you and we call a soul can move on beyond its physical form to inhabit another physical form in the future. Our ability to connect with past souls to know and understand the past is part of this process. From the viewpoint of the soul, it passes on to a future life that is created in time.

So the recollection, then would simply be a recollection of a life lived in another body?

Sometimes there is lingering energy that leaves an imprint that lasts beyond and transcends the travel between the ending of an old life and the beginning of a new one. These imprints can be strong, based on the personality of the life form. Certain dynamic personalities will transcend, allowing a life form to remember faint impressions of the past.

Thank you. Are you familiar with the book we call the Bible and the Book of Genesis?

Yes. It is, in many cultures, an important myth that gives well-being to the cultures that embrace it.

Yes. Many philosophical teachings do provide solace and direction. There is a statement made in Genesis that says 'The Nehalem (sons of God, AKA angels) mated with the daughters of man.' I don't know if the Nehalem are beings from another planet or some other form of being, but you might have some comment on that.

The Nehalem is one form that humans regard as an angel. They are, in fact, early visitors of other beings that came and interacted with humans. What humans interpreted as a form of angel was, in fact, a form of visitor from another planet, long ago.

I would to like ask about what we call the 'white light.' When we human beings get ready to pass over (out of our bodies) we may see a column of white light that we are drawn to and are then lifted up. Of course, there are many stories of human beings being taken up into a beam of light into space ships. Is this simply a coincidence or is there some correlation?

It is a coincidence. The white beam is often used as a transport mechanism to lift beings and humans into a craft. At the end of life, there is another form of light, different, which transports to another dimension, what you call the afterlife. These appear similar, but they are actually two different things. One is the passing of a soul to another life form in another dimension. The other is a technological device, which can seem to mimic that, but it is merely a transport device, remaining in the same dimension. It is used to return the same way. In the afterlife, the movement of the soul is in one direction only.

The Christ energy or the Buddha energy, I assume that they were sent here to help us live more reasonable, loving lives. Did they come only from the human species or were they an intervention from some other kind of life form?

Like the Arc of the Covenant question, the Arc was a portal to another dimension. Religious beliefs are a portal to another dimension also. It would be an interaction between humans and other life forms with an energy that encompasses the Universe. These interactions are interpreted in their own way, each to their own interpretation. It is a larger context of a spiritual concept of a creator. The connection between the two would be both human in origin and nonhuman in origin. It is the energy between each that is the relationship between more 'physical' life forms and higher spiritual forms of energy. It is a difficult concept to define.

Contact

Steve's question: There are stories of human beings being abducted and taken through walls and windows. What mechanism is in place when that occurs?

Many species use a fundamental mechanism for this process, including us. This is a basic mechanism advanced for some species, yet not advanced for us. It is an old way of manipulating matter for covertly abducting humans. There are very few particles in matter that constitutes a solid object. The space between particles of matter can be temporarily shifted in frequency to allow solid masses to pass through other masses that would be interpreted by humans as 'solid' objects.

Is the shift happening with the wall or is it happening with the body?

There is a beam of energy which envelopes the body and the object that the body is to be passed through. Both need to be altered to provide a safe passage through the solid object. Once the body is through the object, the energy that manipulates the matter can be switched off. This is a powerful tool that emanates from the craft. This tool is usually involved in the contact that affords entities and humans unusual abilities to move either into or out of the situations where they are making contact. It provides a level of safety for escape or for entrance into a situation where a human being can be taken. It gives entities with this technology the ability to enter a dwelling and leave safely.

There was a curious incident where an alien being, who would often take this person through a window, took them instead through the front door. There was an indication that there was some problem with taking them through the glass. Perhaps that might be due to some toxic or some other element in the glass. What do you think?

There are certain materials and certain configurations of materials that are less conducive to safe transport than other materials. The large window in this case had a certain elasticity that made exact shifting of frequencies less precise. Much like a finger pressing against a bubble, it was displaced not only in its current difficult configuration, but also in the adjusted new configuration, which made too many unpredictable qualities in the material to afford safe passage. A solid door, though thicker, was a more stable material in which to manipulate frequencies. This is often the case. The grey species use this technology. They often use windows to pass through as a most common entrance and exit. However, the size of the window in that particular case made it safer to pass through the front door.

Here in California, in Phoenix, Arizona, and a few other places, people have been observing extremely large triangular shapes with lights in the sky. They are so large that I don't think that human beings have manufactured them. Are they perhaps holograms or can you tell us to whom they might belong?

The Phoenix lights and other objects are from an advanced species that wishes to demonstrate its presence. They do not necessarily follow a policy of covert interaction with humans. They sometimes wish to demonstrate their technology and great power. These are not our species, but other ones, which also take an interest in Earth. There are a number of species that interact with Earth and with humans. They seem similar in appearance, but a number of their craft are different from ours, and they often have their own agendas when they show off their presence. They seem to be less concerned with non-interference.

I get the sense that they come here on a kind observation tour, almost a holiday-like excursion of Earth, but it might just be my own reaction to it.

We do have times of work and times of rest that often entail traveling for the pleasure of traveling. Work and pleasure are often not as contrasting for us as in your species. Rest is merely a refocusing of the mind to something less demanding, but the mind is still active. Often, there are excursions to far off places to explore and enjoy the other forms of life and the variety of exploring the universe. Vacation is what you are saying. We understand the concept. It is less clearly defined with us, but we understand the concept, particular in humans and in their need to rest and enjoy a sense of play. It is important in the human species to have a balance between rest and work. It is part of human evolution.

The Universe

No questions in this session.

Other

No questions in this session.

Open Session for Comments and Questions

I wish well-being for both Steve and Mary and I enjoy these regular contacts. I hope that Steve will soon find positive energies to continue. He will have many positive things in the near future, and I also wish this for you, Mary. Thank you for this time and these unusual meetings.

Thank you, and until we meet again, good night.

Session VIII, Zetan Society, Light Frequencies
September 18, 2011

Steve was inducted. He begins describing what he sees during the initial induction. For this induction it was suggested to him that he is lying in a hammock in Tahiti. The therapist requested than Han step forward when he is ready to communicate.

Steve: I see him. I'm lying on my hammock in Tahiti. I am now on my side reclining on the hammock. Han is to my right and he is sitting on the sand next to me, next to the hammock. He sits on a mound of black sand. His legs are kind of semi-folded, Indian style. He sits facing me and we are looking at each other. I reach out and we clasp hands, greeting as friends. He takes the other hand and he starts rocking the hammock.

(Therapist laughs.)

Steve: He is like an old pal. He brings his arm back to his lap and he is sort of waiting for the three of us, when it is the appropriate time. It is strange seeing him in this tropical setting, and yet, it is also not strange. Actually, it is very beautiful.

Is he alone this time?

Steve: No. There is another who is sitting Indian style, too. Actually, there are two more. They are sitting Indian style and they are behind him sitting on the sand in the shade in the palm trees. They form a kind of long triangle with two close together, sitting side-by-side in the background. Han is in the front, near me in the hammock. They are rather distant, but they are attentive, should Han call them. That is what is happening.

Well, we welcome them all. Han, are you ready to begin?

Yes.

Earth History

Are you familiar with the term 'Mt. Olympus?'

Yes. It is an old mythology, not by our standards, but old by Earth standards, based in an area of the planet known by you as the Mediterranean.

Did it actually exist, or was it just a good story?

There were contacts with entities and humans. The mythology grew out of that contact. The entities did not intend to become or assume an image of the mythological characters with great powers. It was a good story that grew out of contact with humans and visitors, and then, in passing on the stories over time, with their advanced abilities, they assumed the part of gods.

Hence the name Zeus?

One of many, Zeus, Athena, and others, in various human stories. They are much like the modern superheroes of your present time, with different roles and abilities working together. A class unto themselves, they fired human imagination and gave them a sense that there was something greater than they were that looks over them. There seems to be a human need for this. In many cultures, humans feel that there is something greater than themselves who must control the weather and the stars to give them good crops and abundance of life. The human, who is still culturally growing, looks with the eyes of a child to a mother and father in the sky. It gives them comfort and solace and peace in their own well-being. Often, entities from other worlds inadvertently fulfill this role. Sometimes they do so indirectly. It is part of the human gift for imagination. Imagination is as important as knowledge.

Is imagination not the precursor to creation?

Yes. Without the ability to imagine, one cannot create.

One mystery for mankind has been the following: There have been a number of walls, pyramids, even a castle built with extremely large, heavy stones. Can you tell us what mechanism was used to enable the lifting and placing of these stones? Let's say the pyramids, for instance.

Modern man, in interpreting these structures, often does not comprehend the extent of time spent - the abilities of early man, perhaps assisted by advanced out-world cultures, to create these structures for their own purposes. Many times in history, human knowledge has ebbed and flowed. Many abilities and knowledge are lost, only to be regained later. Often, human pride will mark itself by thinking man has innovated new concepts when actually the concepts may have been used in earlier times just as well. Current humanity is often surprised by the abilities of ancient man that even exceeded what is possible today. The sense of speed in which new modern structures can be built creates a false expectation and belief that earlier structures could not be built just as rapidly. It seems impossible. In fact, many of these structures were very noble designs. Through innovations, both human and non-human assistance was able to help create lasting structures that have withstood the ebb and flow of knowledge of how they were created. They withstand the test of time and entropy, even when the tides of knowledge are lost and then regained. Many physical techniques of advanced tooling, levers, and gravity used in an elaborate fashion made these ancient structures a reality.

There was alien assistance in supplying tools that were harder than the substances being fashioned. We have been able to provide, without humans knowing, certain assistance in their construction. We enjoy watching humans create their structures. It was an expression and a test of their knowledge. This partial assistance gives us a gauge in understanding the limits of their development over time.

Using alien technology, does that include using specific materials to enable easier lifting, for example, Coral Castle? It was noted that a certain coral was used for building blocks. The Latvian-American Edward Leedskalnin managed to lift these blocks and built the castle by himself. If he had used different materials, would it have presented different problems in lifting them?

If I understand, coral was used as part of a mixture, like concrete, to help develop a rigid, strong structure. Coral could have been used in this.

Yes. It could have been added, but I think the castle I am referring to in Florida had huge blocks of coral, placed one on top of another without anything in between the stones. Would coral have been easier to lift because of its properties than perhaps some other kind of stone?

Our understanding of coral is that it is very strong with sometimes brittle characteristics. One of its features is that it is not as dense and maybe, with proper care, would have been easier to transport in order to position where it could best benefit the structure. It has many open pores and elements that make it light and strong, like a sponge, but like a hard sponge, rigid. This is well known already. It would be easier to move in certain construction settings.

Perhaps the individual who moved these stones used something akin to humans sitting around a table, placing their hands on a table, creating a vibration in the table and the table sometimes lifting of its own accord. Could that be a type of system that might be used for lifting?

We use certain telepathic energies to levitate. This is possible. It may have been used in this situation.

Can you tell us something about the origin and purpose of the place we call Stonehenge?

Stonehenge is well known to us. Many crop circles are created near this situation. It is a source of energy and magnetic fields based on the mineral content in the soil. It acts as a kind of lighthouse or navigation beacon for us in navigating to this planet or navigating within this planet. When you mention Stonehenge, a smile comes to me because of my familiar acquaintance with it. It is an ancient calendar sitting on top of an energy engine that comes from within the Earth itself that is a source of such magnetic fields. It is interesting that humans had been fortuitous enough to place Stonehenge in that location underneath such a beacon that we use.

Some humans are sensitive to the Earth field energies.

That is correct, the Earth field energies.

Have you ever heard of a place called Hyperborean, a land with 24 hour-a-day sunshine?

No.

Are you familiar with a being known as Enoch? He was apparently contacted by some higher order being who took him on a tour of the heavens and other realities. The book concerning his travels was written by an order called The White Brotherhood.

No.

Do you know of the statues on a place called Easter Island?

Yes.

Can you tell us anything about those statues?

They are one more of a kind of homage by man to the sky and those who came from the sky. Many of the edifices on Easter Island are radioactive. Others are not. They come from a place on the island where, surprisingly, certain areas have many uranium deposits. All building materials came from a small proximity to the original basin. This is the area of the ground where the stones were originally extracted and transported.

They have been radioactive for many years. These are from the natural deposits. Some form invisible markers for us as natural wave points. They emanate energies that are not well known to humans, but they help us to navigate.

At an earlier time to the monument building, other cultures migrated to this place you call Easter Island. Like the Atlantis that we discussed earlier, so there was another advanced culture on that island, too, independent of the earlier discussion about Atlantis. In several places around the Earth, in Europe, the Mediterranean and South America, there were many advanced cultures that independently developed on islands apart from the main continents. These cultures, when the right conditions existed for life and intellectual development, were able to create a great abundance of knowledge, information, and abilities to accomplish certain astonishing tasks by human standards.

Thank you. The radioactivity was a surprise.

Is the Earth in a state of global warming or is it simply getting ready to move into a small ice age?

The Earth moves through climate cycles. We have noticed this on other planets as well. Part of this is due to the star and part is due to the local climatic conditions on any planet. Earth is at a warming and then cooling cycle. It is anticipated that the Earth will go through a warming cycle. This in turn will reduce the polar caps and create more water surface area. This in turn will cool the planet, resulting in the initiation and acceleration of a not-too extensive minor ice age.

Are we talking hundreds of years here or thousands of years?

In thousands of years. It is the normal cycle. The cycle, however, has been accelerated by man's influence on the planet. His technology accelerates the heating and cooling process, making this warming period more acute than others and creating more rapid change. This is due to the technology developed by man in the last 150 years.

You are familiar with the Aborigines in Australia. I understand that when they miss someone who has gone far away and they want them to come home, they 'sing' them home, using their telepathic abilities. Are you familiar with this kind of musical telepathy?

The Aborigines are like our cousins in the way we regard them. It is ironic that they are often regarded by their fellow human cultures as very primitive. We regard them as very advanced. This irony would astonish other humans. They are more akin to us and similar to us in how we communicate with and reach out to others and our communities across space. In a greater sense, it is with affection that we see the Aborigines as telepathically more advanced than other humans on your planet.

I see their advancement not only in being telepathic, but also in their living with Earth in a sustainable way, living easily with nature, without the heavy carbon footprint of many other cultures.

They live simply. It is a way that is in harmony with the planet, like many other so-called primitive cultures. Native Americans regard the Earth as their Mother in their culture, as do the Aborigines. They are part of the land. They do not feel they are possessive of certain lands. They are part of the land and the land is part of them. They are at one in the relationship. It is not dissimilar on other planets and in other cultures. They do not have certain advantages in technology, but they are advanced in other ways. Our culture, in a way, reflects both. Some Earth cultures use the telepathic connection while others use technology. Our culture is able to integrate both of these assets into one. In a way, it helps define who we are. It is with respect and affection that we see the Aborigines, in many ways, as an advanced life form, compared to those around them who do not regard them in the same way. This is part of the way of humanity. In time, an amalgamation of various values will create a form of human that will integrate all these strengths and values.

Could you tell us about the origin and purpose of the crystal skulls? At present we believe there are 12 or 13 skulls.

They are used to resonate certain energy fields. They were created by non-human sources. The ability to create such skulls in such a manner is beyond early man's ability. They had assistance. They act as a kind of device to collect and focus certain energies surrounding the Earth for purposes as yet undisclosed. These energies were used in the past and can be relevant for the present and future.

Apparently, there have been some instances of healing in the presence of one or more of these stones.

This is one of many ways this energy manifests itself through these crystals.

Zeta Reticuli History

What does your culture value most?

We value knowledge and exploration. We are primarily explorers, but we are also nurturers of new life and new places. We strive to develop comfortable living areas on planets for the successful advancement of societies. We feel like we are developers as well as explorers. We take pride in this. It is not one where we are displacing one culture for another. It is not a hostile advancement. It is just the natural advancement of a species over many places of the galaxy that have the room for living space. We do not displace our culture for another or dominate one. There is plenty of room for all and the ability to travel great distances is just as easy as traveling relatively short distances. There is plenty for trade, exchange of ideas, information, and material things that each need and share in their development.

Does your species use lasers?

The amplification of light frequencies is used as a tool in many things such as communication, transportation, and measurement. Like many light sources or energies, these are often beamed from craft to transport our beings and other beings with similar abilities. Often, seen by humans as a great white light, it is a form of technology used for short distant transport. Forms of lasers are also used for discrete communication, where signals are not broadcast randomly, but are sent to specific destinations for discrete communication between species and spacecraft. It is also used in many tools for healing and surgeries.

Many species use similar devices for healing or for dissection of animals and other tasks. Lasers are also used as a source for creating primitive fusion. This, in time, humans will learn about themselves. There will be a point where more energy will be created, but it will take more time before humans have the ability to create a small sun and fusion energy. This will take much time.

Just a little question about your biology. In the diet you described, did you evolve beyond needing to have teeth?

We do have a type of teeth. They are smaller and there are more of them, compared to human teeth. They are used for mastication. Our mouth is small, and we have a long slim neck. It is important that food be masticated thoroughly to enable swallowing it down a slim esophagus and then down into the body. The teeth are not used anywhere for aggressive purposes. Maybe they were used defensively when we were a primitive life form. We evolved into the state we are now. Our mouths have changed to enable a more suitable diet of liquids, soft foods, fruits, and vegetables from various places. Apples are a delicacy that we enjoy. Earth is the source of apples for us, including many other good things and we have transplanted these to other worlds. We associate Earth with many good things.

Spirituality

How does your species perceive species with greater intelligence than yourselves?

We mark our place and have consideration of civilizations that are less advanced than we are. We are mindful of them when we make contact with higher advanced forms. We understand that higher order beings often do not share certain things, but only do so at certain times when it is appropriate for us to advance ourselves. In exchange, we pass that policy down in our contact with less advanced forms. We are mindful of how life and cultures develop. We have often seen advanced forms where they evolve beyond physical instrumentalities. We have many abilities to communicate telepathically across great distances, planet to planet and across the land on our planet, or within this planet (Earth), but we are limited to certain physical material limitations.

Many advanced forms have achieved a merging of energy where they are a consciousness enveloped in energy and have the ability to travel almost instantly, in almost an omnipresent way about the Universe. This is what some humans would regard as God. While we feel that there are higher advanced spiritual forms, these were actually former life forms like us who have evolved to an even higher level where they have become energy and light. They have become so intimately interconnected with the forces of the Universe that certain processes in the Universe incorporate their higher intelligence and wisdom. This is a great mystery to us, too. They can create in a way that astonishes and mystifies us and they can become one with the great powers and abilities that create the processes of the Universe. With their intelligence, they use the basic forms of matter of the Universe as their clay to create on a level that is incomprehensible even to us.

Do you think that their greater intelligence has made them more compassionate?

They have become both more compassionate and less compassionate. They are more compassionate in a broader sense, but less compassionate for the individual because their scope and vision does not incorporate individual planets and the individual life form. These advanced spiritual energy life forms are symbiotic, with physically advanced life forms, in assisting or accelerating the natural process of life in the Universe.

This natural process begins with raw matter created within stars and evolves into the raw matter of advanced intelligence that comprehends and is self-aware everywhere. Everything in the Universe, from the most fundamental to the most spiritually advanced life energies is all part of a greater Universal ecology, each with an important part to contribute.

Contact

You probably know of the species that we call Anunnaki. Do you know why they came to Earth?

The Anunnaki are part of ongoing, continuous contact at various times with various out-world civilizations. They provided early technology and skills to enhance the skills that humans already possessed and combined them. This created some remarkable feats.

Were they interested in any minerals on our planet?

Yes, in exchange. They were interested in many ores, including gold and other minerals, for use in forming their technology in their craft and other instrumentalities. Gold is an excellent conductor. The Anunnaki do not have the mineral material wealth that Earth does. The minerals provide a technological means. It is used for technological purposes. I suppose that creates its own value.

Were there any particular stones in which they were interested?

Not in particular, other than it was just required for breaking down minerals into their basic compounds and elements for use in manufacturing in Anunnaki technology. In exchange, out of gratitude, the Anunnaki provided comfort, security, and certain tools that enabled man to live a more comfortable life. The Anunnaki are very considerate and fair-minded in any exchange, though they do have a reputation for exploiting primitive life forms.

Are they still coming to this planet?

Yes, but in a discreet fashion, not so overtly. This is one of their way stations.

Outside of Santa Fe, New Mexico, I observed an unusual conglomeration of lights in the sky over the low-lying hills. Are there any underground facilities there that are not man made?

There are regions of New Mexico, due to their remoteness, which are used. The hidden facilities, that are not man made, are often used as places for unknown purposes, much the way craft can pass through solid matter and mountains. I spoke of this much earlier in our discussions. Many of these underground areas are in New Mexico, particularly Dulce and to the north of Dulce. Many humans, with a higher sense of perception, have congregated in these areas, sensing beyond the normal human ability. They, too, realize there is significance to these areas. It is interesting that, later, many atomic tests were done in other areas in the vicinity, hundreds of miles away, but still in what humans call the neighborhood.

As you probably have heard, New Mexico is called the 'Land of Enchantment' and anyone who is paying attention, senses a shift in vibration and almost a kind of excitement and awe. It seems to be quite a special place.

Our telepathic abilities also notice this, to an even greater degree. It is a natural haven for much energy. Much like certain humans go to warm places to relax, we go to places, such as Dulce, due to the energy fields that seem to emanate from there. It is on a wavelength beyond some humans, but not as few as they suspect. They may unconsciously congregate there for reasons that they do not understand, but the same energies that draw them that also draw us. New Mexico is a special place.

The Universe

Please describe the culture of another human species that lives in our galaxy.

There is a strain of humanoid that often is interpreted by humans on this planet as the Nordics, due to their skin and hair color. It is a species that is very handsome by some standards. They are part of the larger community of life in the Universe. They also often interact with humans. One who was called Travis Walton, a contactee, had an encounter. He encountered greys and the Nordics. It was a Nordic who was able to make Mr. Walton comfortable in his stressful situation during his encounter.

How would you describe the Nordic's cultural outlook?

They are an advanced culture, compared to Earth culture. Nordics are between humans and us. They have the ability of interstellar travel and use it quite readily. Their culture might be considered a utopia by Earth standards. They also have their deficiencies. They have increased to a level where their life and their energies encompass whole star systems now. Instead of just energy sources from a planet, they have achieved a higher level of technology and infrastructure so that they live abundantly on many planets. Their societies seem to promote well-being and a sense of pride. This is difficult to describe. Using a trait of humans, I think it could be described as Nordics being enamored with themselves. Vain? There is a sense of pride in themselves and in their culture that can be disconcerting to other cultures, but it is tolerated. They are very impressed with themselves. This would be a good term to use.

What do they value most in their culture?

They value a sense of beauty, aesthetics, and wealth in providing a good foundation for their culture. They feel they are very successful. They have a sense of pride in their achievements.

Other

No questions in this session.

Open Session for Comments or Questions

Is there anything that you want to talk about or add as we start to move this session toward its close, including your friends?

Our friends have sat silently in the back. They wish to monitor the contact. They see that it is beneficial and encourage further contact. They give their approval. They are comfortable with the setting and enjoy contact with you, Mary and with you, Steve. Steve is going through a time of great transition. He has been a useful conduit for this communication. We are mindful of the changes he is going through and his life will be different in a positive way. We suggest that he hold fast, be patient, and look to his hope and faith in the future. We also wish this for you, Mary. These are wonderful times and we look forward to further communication. That is all I have to wish for now.

Thank you. We are very grateful. Until the next time.

Session IX, SETI, Ancient Aliens, Biology of Zetans
September 26, 2011

Induction begins. As Steve is beginning the induction process, Han is invited to choose the place of the meeting. Steve begins describing what he sees.

Steve: Oh, there are beautiful colors, all around and to the side. We are on a sandy beach next to a stream. The canyon provides isolation and it is safe for us, all alone. It is a place hard to get to by man.

Is it day or nighttime?

Steve: It is late morning, and we are in the shadow, in the cool shadow of the canyon walls. You look up and the sky is vivid blue and clear. It's warm. I can hear the stream next to us, going through the canyon. I see the soft beaches along the side of the stream. It's lower in the stream and we are sitting together on the beach. The canyon walls are red, orange, and sand. It creates this cathedral like feeling around us. We feel so cool and protected, where no one can interfere, and we can be alone. No hikers will stumble onto us. Han feels protected here and I feel very privileged to be here with him. There is another being with him in the background. They seem to be telepathically connected. The other aliens are here not because they don't trust Han. It's just their nature. Everyone is with everybody else, so their idea of privacy is different from ours. The fact that others are here is of no consequence. It just gives them a sense of belonging and safety being on another planet. You might say a 'buddy' system, even for them.

Steve: It's a sacred place for Native Americans. It is also a sacred place for Han. He likes the serenity and solitude here. There is a silence that is not only appealing to humans, but also appealing to Han. He is telepathically attuned. In this place he can feel alone in his thoughts, meditate, and focus on things far beyond. Here he feels at one with the Universe. It is a meditation place for him. Of all the many places Han could choose in the Universe, he chooses this special place.

Therapist requested that Han step forward when he is ready to communicate.

I am ready.

Earth History

In 1977, our array known as SETI detected a large radio wave. Do you have any idea of its source? Secondly, should we be looking at radio waves as a form of communication between planets?

Radio waves are a natural part of the Universe. It is a form of energy that radiates out, some in natural forms and some in unnatural forms, created by different species. At some point, radio waves are considered quaint and primitive. For some advanced forms capable of what humans would call long distance space flight, it might be overlooked or forgotten. In SETI's case, they eventually discover an unnatural source of radio waves, one that does not follow the natural cycle or rhythm. This could indicate intelligent life, but it is like holding a candle next to a star. There are so many other wavelengths and means of communication. It is primitive. Not wishing to be rude or unflattering, but SETI is, at this point, not practical. However, it is a human beginning. It also expresses the human desire to be connected with other life in the Universe, which abounds also on Earth. It is not capable or efficient in quick, timely communication. It would take many years and decades for an exchange of conversation. There are means, now faster than light, a physical means, and a telepathic means, where it is possible to communicate, but SETI is an early crude attempt. It might be more a random chance. There is a term you call 'luck' that something will be found. For the most part, life forms of an advanced nature are aware of other life that is less advanced. We have developed forms of communication between advanced forms that are more discrete and prevent random contact, in mindful consideration of the development of less advanced beings.

The technology, aside from telepathy, is it based on light?

The human advanced theoretical physicists are only now beginning to comprehend light and other energies. Another energy, gravity, contains relevant properties. Once humans have understood the properties of gravity waves and that gravity can be folded in on itself, what will be revealed will result in a far higher form of technology. Man will become capable of travel between stars and galaxies and will communicate through thought, almost instantaneously. It is based on the broad concept of a deeper underlying resonance that exists throughout the physical Universe. It will be gravity waves traveling faster-than-light, not light energies, which will facilitate such communication and transportation. Much of this must seem astonishing to you. We commend the human desire to connect to us. SETI is a primitive first step. The desire to be drawn to the sky and stars is the correct and noble one in your evolution.

Zeta Reticuli History

What mechanism or means do you use for the storage of knowledge or information that you want to keep indefinitely?

We have forms of light and energy, which can be contained to hold vast quantities of knowledge. In human cultural mythology, light is often symbolic for knowledge. This is literally true in our culture. We have forms of data and knowledge storage in light that is contained within certain forms that hold vast quantities of knowledge. Within these physical forms, much like the electrical exchanges within the human brain, knowledge is kept in memory, when not in use. We, in a similar fashion, store, on a larger scale, light energy and electrical impulses within forms of plasma energies. It is a more efficient use of energy and knowledge. This enables vast knowledge to be saved in a smaller space.

This stored knowledge that we have accumulated supplements the existing higher order of thought shared telepathically within our species' society, the community of mind. The social knowledge between our species is saved on an organic level, through our closely connected telepathic community.

There are certain fundamental concepts and knowledge that make us, as a species, who we are. Our identity has been saved in a material sense, like your libraries. Humans form repositories of knowledge. We, too, have libraries. These provide a backup and redundancy. If our race should somehow be extinguished, the knowledge will continue and if survivors need to access, it will be available.

In your skeletal structure, are your bones, rounded or flat? Are they cartilage-like? How are they different from ours?

We have, in some ways, cartilage type structures and yet, at the same time, we have bone structures, which have been adapted. Our evolution came from a being, our missing link, that you might say was a type of humanoid bird. To fly, this bird needed hollow bones. Over time, these bones, which were light and strong in structure for flight, adapted to become appropriate for land beings, as we appear today as a species. We genetically enhanced our bone structure for greater density strength. We also have a structure that interweaves with a type of biological fabric that gives added strength and lightness to us. The lightness came from our long ago, bird-like bone structure, but in time, a type of weave-like structural fabric adapted to these bones to give them strength. They seem quite small and frail, great strength, as compared to human bones.

It reminds me a little bit of a material we developed call Kevlar.

Yes. This is a very good analogy. It is like a type of crude material you call fiberglass. There is a resin with a cloth weave. In a way, evolution has provided us with an additional organic cloth weave for greater strength, much like Kevlar.

I assume that your species has a certain amount of habitat under water. If that is the case, have you found a way to breathe in the water or do you live solely in a habitat that has the proper atmosphere mix?

It is easy for us to create habitats under water, as you refer to them, immersed in our planet's oceans. We also use these habitats on Earth to conceal our presence to provide temporary 'way points' beyond the awareness of humans. We use these habitats. We do not have the ability to breathe underwater due to our biology, but we have the ability to adapt, in a sense, swim in the oceans. It requires some apparatus to do this. It is not like the oxygen that humans often carry, but we have the ability to absorb oxygen through adaptation.

What is the appropriate chemical mix for you to breathe?

It is somewhat similar to yours. It has some variations. It is nitrogen and oxygen in slightly different proportions, but within livable ratios. In the ocean, our bodies often have more difficulty coping with the pressures. Often, parts of our bodies have certain pockets that can be a hindrance in coping with such pressures, but we can create fields around us, much like our ships, when traveling through the oceans and through the Earth's atmosphere. This provides a protective field to cope with those pressures. This provides a kind of invisible diving suit you might say, in which we can swim in a protective bubble where the pressure is acceptable for our life forms. We are not good swimmers, compared to humans, but we can exist in this liquid. We mainly use these habitats to exist within water and they allow us to explore areas of this planet still beyond the reach of human technology at the present time.

Concerning life expectancy, is your life expectancy a thousand years or so?

I am conferring with my other friend. Yes. It is acceptable to talk about this.

My question is actually an extension beyond that question.

Our life expectancy is 1,000 to 1,500 years in Earth time.

Considering this, and the short human life expectancy, do you think we are more driven to look at our spiritual aspect because our of short life spans, whereas your species may be less driven to look at your spiritual aspect because of your very long life spans?

The concept of time is relevant to each species. What is short to one may be long to another, but it is still time. In relative terms, perhaps we have more time to contemplate a spiritual afterlife that we also believe in. It is part of the greater consciousness. Humans also share in a form of the same thing. The seeming short time to one also seems short to the other. The wish to survive and cling to life is a fundamental drive and instinct of all living forms, regardless of time. Human life seems short in comparison to us, but this has been of benefit to them in the greater evolutionary path for adaptation.

Humans, as well as our own species, may feel cheated and it is each to their own to make life as full as they can within their individual periods of time, whether considered long or short. There are life forms that live even beyond our life span. In a sense, we also have a sense of envy that they live longer. We can understand the concept. The wish for all life forms is to live fully and productively. You form a sense of connective-ness to the greater mystery of life that is part of our consciousness, too. It should be one to desire a higher quality of life, however long the quantity of life may be.

Concerning deviant thoughts and behaviors, without assigning 'good' or 'bad' judgments, how does your species handle deviant thoughts or behavior?

We can become quickly aware of deviant thought. Within the fabric of our community of mind, even our species sometimes requires specialized scientists to deal with the physical health of our species, often requiring cures.

Are you saying that chemical and biological differences create deviant behavior?

Yes. In human terms, mental illness is a plague that encompasses a small degree of human consciousness. We have often encountered this in our contact with humans. By comparing various impressions with other human contacts, these impressions amalgamate, enabling us to see this in a larger perspective. It is also so with other species. Due to the mental abilities of our species, mental illness can be more acute and of great concern. At the same time, the interconnective weave makes it much more quickly apparent and can be treated as such. Deviant behavior is defined in our values. It causes harm to others around them. Sometimes deviant behavior in its milder form can just be exploring a new life behavior which, within our social fabric we can tolerate. If it extends to where it harms others mentally or physically and causes cruelty, then this needs to be addressed within the social fabric of our society.

Thank you. I do believe a little deviance is probably healthy so that one can explore a little, stretch a little, and then evaluate. However, I do understand that excessive deviance can have a much greater effect in your culture than it would in ours.

It creates diversity. When a different type of behavior, within the confines of interacting with other life, is expressed in kindness in the normal expected exchange between life forms, it is tolerated. Some so-called deviance is welcome and is inconsequential to the greater variety and enrichment of our social behavior.

Has your species evolved beyond needing any specialized defenses?

In a biological sense or in a military sense?

Let's say military sense for this question.

We do have the capabilities to protect ourselves against species on our same level of evolution. However, it is a matter of diverting energy to other tasks. It is not the specialized apparatus that is required which often wastes resources and time to develop technologies. Instead, we can use energy and matter that can be diverted quickly, if need arises. Otherwise, the material for military offense or defense does not require large stockpiles of materials to make this possible. It can be created quickly. In the greater context of life, it is not necessary.

My hope was that a species that has reached your level of knowledge would no longer need military means.

In the network of life, most of our neighbors are aware of each other. We interact peaceably. The capability exists, but it is not needed. Nevertheless, should an unknown force come within our region that does not hold our values, we could collectively develop that capability. At our current level of understanding this need does not exist. The best we understand it, your term 'politics' is a unique human form of orchestrating selfishness. This originates from living on a planet of abundant, but still limited resources and space. We understand this concept from interacting with your world. Advanced intelligent life is connected telepathically within a larger community where understanding and plenty exists, making military forms of interaction unnecessary.

Would it be all right for Steve to draw a simple star map indicating your point of origin in Zeta Reticuli? Please just imprint the map. Steve has a good visual mind.

I can attempt to do so. I am putting an image into his mind. It will take some time. He needs certain precise details. He is slow to take it, but it will be imprinted. I have shown him where his star is and where our binary stars are and the distance in light years. I think I have something for him now. He has that noted.

If you decide to terraform a planet, how do you choose that planet? What are the criteria?

There are many criteria. Some are very complex. Not all can be terraformed. The energy expended is often not worth the effort for such change. There are certain ideals that we look for, certain distances between stars and planets, a habitable zone, as humans call it, that provide a range in which terraforming is more practical. It also has to have certain iron and other material deposits to provide certain gravity. In addition, certain material means are required that could be converted into habitable materials that we recognize. Often, terraforming is just accelerating the natural evolutionary process. Often, certain planets, due to their location, are more desirable, even if they have qualities that make them more difficult to terraform.

Location?

Location. A strategic position for either trade or communication. Often, other forms can be used for terraforming to provide a place. Terraforming is to provide more dwelling space for both us and other species.

Yes. I would think that the next huge evolutionary hurdle for your species might be moving away from the physical and into the nonphysical, but I am just surmising at this point.

We hope so. We feel we have observed higher forms. It is a conceptual state that will take a much longer time to obtain. We feel, if we are worthy in the eyes of those around us and our ultimate creator, we will be worthy of this. Hopefully, we will be a species that is compassionate and at one in peace and harmony with the Universe. We hope that will eventually make us a candidate for a higher spiritual, nonphysical life form. We may eventually attain that. Time will tell. It will take a longer length of time, compared to the human state of rapid development. In many ways, evolution in the Universe creates primitive forms that change into self-aware beings. Intelligent individual life then evolves into a higher, interconnective social consciousness. Evolution is often rapid in the beginning, and like the creation of the Universe, it begins to slow down through entropy. In a way, evolution follows a similar rapid evolutionary development that spreads out broadly like a river.

Spirituality

No questions in this session.

Contact

Steve specifically wanted to know if human beings, when abducted, are monitored afterwards.

Yes, they are monitored by the entities that conduct these illegal actions. They want to know where they are so they can be located quickly for later contacts to monitor their progress and to be able to return for additional genetic material or whatever function these entities wish. They often implant these humans in discrete places with psychotronic devices not recognized by humans as such. This is part of their covert process. Humans are intelligent enough to recognize these devices. *The greatest advantage these criminal entities have is the great disbelief that Earth-centered humans maintain and their refusal to accept that these events occur.* In a way, this makes their work easier. The greatest veil is from the human source and the humans' inability to accept that contact is occurring, legally or illegally.

The implants do not send out a signal. They merely enhance the brainwave frequencies that already organically exist in the abductee. An implant acts as an amplifier for these entities to pick up the radiating brainwave frequencies, each with their own unique identity. These provide a quick and clear identify-cation from a reasonable distance away.

The detection of signals of the human mind is not across distant space, but across hundreds of miles. Human minds, amplified by these implants, betray their presence to these criminals who perform these acts for selfish reasons. They do not respect humans. In a sense, we, too, have made contact with humans, much in the way we are now, but also in a setting that might be interpreted as an abduction. However, it is often to impart knowledge and to educate certain individuals whom we feel have potential for high clairvoyance and a sense of purpose and destiny. We give them help to steer humanity in a direction that would eventually bring inter-consecutiveness between life forms.

I think we may know one of these individuals. Are you familiar with a being known as George LoBuono, a telepath who communicates with various alien species? (George is the author of the book, Alien Mind.)

Yes. He is an old friend. He is one of several people in that geographic area who often exchange ideas and communication. He is a very interesting and sophisticated communicator. He has learned well how to exchange ideas with us. He understands and participates in multiple levels of exchange simultaneously, much like our means of com-municating. The communication I give to your client is on a higher, but still a relatively unsophisticated level at a speed that he can accept and pass on. George has had more training and experience to make multiple levels of communication possible. It's like Steve is a two-lane, and George is a four-lane on your road structures on your planet in which more traffic can be exchanged at the same rate of speed. George is a good fellow. Often, some entities are not comfortable with what he shares in his writings, and others are very happy with that. Let him know that. The entities that he comes in contact with, they mean well, and they know that his intentions are good for opening an avenue for exchange. Others (humans) could also become involved if they were not so self-conscious. They could become aware of the higher possibilities around them. They could easily communicate with us in the same way, if they were so inclined. George is able to do this, and he is ahead in that respect.

Many years ago when I was in a state of mediation or prayer, I had the distinct feeling, a kind of visual feeling, that I was being downloaded with a stream of symbols that came very fast. I suspect their source was off-world. Is that one of the ways that information is passed very quickly – in symbolic streams?

Yes. The importance is to retain what is sent to that person, at some level. Humans respond easily to symbols and visual forms. In meditation, there is a sense of well-being and beauty that comes over Mary that is quite remarkable. It is a sense that she is being open and receptive to much that is beyond in many dimensions in this Universe. She is a remarkable person who feels and understands there is much beyond her and this physical world and is in contact with it. This is beyond most of her fellow people. They do not comprehend. Many often underestimate what exists, but Mary has a gift. She uses the gifts bestowed upon her. This allows her, at some level, to retain the many forms of symbols sent to her. Often these can be mathematical or symbols of life experiences. These can be imprinted on more people, if they are receptive.

Would these contacts have come from a specific star system?

I keep seeing the Pleiades. I just see a group of stars in a magical swarm like bees, and I recognize them as the Pleiades. I am not surprised that the entities from there would do this.

They have abilities to do this. Some are higher advanced forms that even our species. Know that their intentions are wise and good, and there is nothing to fear from them. They have wisdom and insights similar to ours, but in some ways, they are more advanced and, as such, we respect that. The Pleiades seem to be one of several places that these entities exist, but their main home comes from what humans call the Pleiades.

Thank you. Concerning the program that is called Serpo, I understand that it is still ongoing, and that there is still an exchange of human beings and non-Earth life forms. Can you tell me when the last exchange took place?

The last occurred in human timeline in the 1980s. This exchange is still ongoing today, but after the 1980s, the method changed. There were long-term visits and exchanges between our civilization and Earth civilization. Many of the humans who lived on the planet had emotional difficulty in living away from Earth. There is a sense of interconnectiveness that we also understand in our species.

In many ways, humans function primarily as individuals. This makes them both admirable and dangerous because they do not have a group mentality and a sense of all things and values that interconnect them. Individuals can often act rashly.

We discovered that humans, too, have a subconscious sense of belonging and interconnectiveness. They underestimated this sense of belonging and, therefore, they did not realize that homesickness would affect them on a deeply emotional level in a very basic and fundamental way. They underestimated the emotional impact.

In learning to travel through space, humans will learn not only the physiological, but also the emotional challenges of space flight. It will help them focus on what life is and what it means to each one. The challenge of space flight will bring these into focus and ultimately help, in the end, to provide great growth in an evolutionary way as humans meet these challenges on very physical, emotional, and spiritual levels. Serpo was a partial success. Later, in the 1980s, the conditions of the experiment were changed and modified to accommodate these unanticipated shortcomings in the eventual growth of humans in their sense of what makes them who they are. We modified the experiment for shorter visits so that they could return back to their kind for re-energizing their well-being and state-of-mind. Being so interconnected, we understand this need. Therefore, in consideration, the exchange times were shortened greatly. In Earth years, exchanges were reduced to a matter of weeks and months.

How many have been exchanged?

Cumulatively, several hundred, in groups of 12 or more.

How are they faring now that they have been returned?

Their lives are changed. Their outlook has been broadened so much. At the same time, due to certain social and political constraints of human Earth societies, they are isolated, unable to share their impressions for fear of how their fellow humans will react to new perspectives. A conflict can form between old ways and new ways and views, ones that are closer to the truth in a broader, larger sense. However, there is a human quality, often like stubbornness, the unwillingness to change to new ideas. In a way, it is ironic and sad that many who returned with such great knowledge and broadened perspectives are unable to share. They are frustrated because they have been isolated and unable to share their experiences. Part of my work here and the work of others is to relax their feelings that they must be isolated and frustrated in not being able to share with other humans the knowledge shown to them.

Hopefully, they are being introduced to people who can accept them with their experiences. I know that I am certainly willing to talk with them and I hope there are many others out there who are willing to talk to them and not judge them.

A curious quality about humans results from their inability to normally exchange telepathically. One human writer said, 'No man is an island.' However, in one way, each human being is an island in and unto himself. This is a strange concept to us who come from a society where everyone feels part of the other in a conscious way.

I look at the concept of aloneness,, and I see it as a kind of strange gift because that sense of being alone makes us fight back to find a place where we know we are not alone. It is almost as though we were born here in ignorance, and part of our evolution is to find out, in fact, we are not an island.

Ultimately, humans will learn that quality. When that happens, your planet will change in many fundamental ways. Hostility will decrease between groups of humans and tolerance will increase. Understanding will greatly increase between groups. When humans are shown such knowledge and then put in isolation on their planet to control that knowledge, it can seem frustrating to us. The knowledge is only put out slowly, measure-by-measure, to integrate the knowledge into human culture. We also understand the human sense of continuity and often the resistance to change.

Yes. It is that desire for predictability.

So, we are patient, and in a larger context, we have been around a long time. We are aware of the sense of struggle that each individual has, combined with the shorter span of life that we often observe on your planet. This provides great diversity and adaptability. It may seem to humans that, in a way, our evolution has slowed down, while human development is at a rapid pace. Perhaps at one time, our own species also were this way and had a rapid development because of a sense of individuality. Along with this individuality can come strife. There are also great strides forward. It is part of the struggle of life, to rise to the top. This we understand. Our species has climbed to a plateau where our evolution is now slower, but there is also a sense of contentment and acceptance of where we are at this moment.

The Universe

What is the nature of consciousness?

Consciousness is an attribute of intelligent beings who are self-aware of their surroundings, not only in a physical sense, but also in a spiritual and telepathic sense, beyond human comprehension. There is much beyond for humans to enjoy and understand. It is a feeling of wellness and consciousness of all that is around you. Full consciousness means being one with the atoms, the bosons, and the elements, in their most fundamental nature, that compose the Universe and of which we are also a part. We are the consciousness of the Universe. This is self-awareness that can understand its beauty and mystery. It is the consciousness of all other consciousness' also reaching out and touching one another, whether near or far, one with each other, in an intimate way, that defies human description. In time, humans will learn to do this as well. Humans have great potential and are like young children, which we were once also. We are like young adults, in comparison. One day, you, too, will enjoy this sense of consciousness and well-being. It is what creates tolerance, peace, love, and understanding across life around the Universe, at its most fundamental level.

Thank you. You are probably familiar with the term 'entanglement' that we use in physics and also the concept of 'intention.' My understanding of 'entanglement' is that close proximity is not required. Even at great distances, there can be exchange at the lowest subatomic particle level and that 'intention' is tied to this process. Would you comment on these concepts?

These are concepts in your notion of quantum physics that would seem strange to most humans. There is the ability to connect across distances and to find a connection where there is no physical connection, yet there is a sense of consciousness there. It is a type of physical phenomenon in physics that, as fantastic as it may seem to humans, is still a well-established fact. This provides connection across distances between certain physical processes in the Universe and between life forms.

Would you describe our meetings together as a reflection of those concepts, among other things?

In a way, yes, this is a form of communication, with not only our minds, but also where our whole beings are drawn and linked in a temporary fashion for communication at these meetings. The setting I chose in the southwest desert is a physical place. It is also a place within our minds that I have suggested. We have created this mind-place between the three of us. It is a setting where there is a sense of solitude, privacy, and well-being. It is a comfortable place for my guests where we can conduct an exchange of knowledge, information, and friendship. This is one means or use for such a telepathic process that you described. It is a way to communicate across our vast distances as well.

Yes, I am familiar with the process of co-creation using thoughts and since I am already familiar with the American Southwest, I found your choice of meeting place quite beautiful. Thank you.

New Mexico, Arizona, and Utah possess the qualities that you describe. It also makes our communication together that much easier and more comfortable for all of us, enriching the process. You are my guests.

Steve would like to know what happens when two galaxies collide.

There is a tremendous interaction on a vast level that most humans cannot comprehend. It is often seen as an ominous thing, but it is both. In human values, it is both to be feared and to be welcomed. In the interaction between two separate galaxies, often the space between stars and planets and many structures that you still have yet to learn about, interact like two ghosts passing through each other. In many ways, some passages are not of consequence to each other because it has such a small effect when comprehended in relation to a galaxy. However, there are also elements of the galaxies that can have ominous consequences for the rest of the galaxy. There is a black hole in each galaxy, holding the galaxy structure in place. The collision of the black holes can have great effect to where, due to the physics of space, one galaxy may end up prevailing over another galaxy.

Some galaxies will pick up elements of the other galaxy as they travel through both space and time. Often, on an individual star and planet level, some planets and stars will be disrupted in their paths and gravitational patterns. These can be of tremendous consequences to the life forms on these planets. Often, these happen on a level where it takes many millions of years in Earth time for galaxies to interact. It may even take billions of years so that the individual life forms on these planets do not often feel the effects, both in time and in physical effects. The Milky Way, as you call it, is our galaxy. At this moment, our Milky Way galaxy is interacting with another galaxy. This is not well known to humans and it is not of any concern or consequence. It is part of the natural state of galaxy interactions.

Has Mars moved beyond an appropriate evolutionary state for terraforming? Has it already bypassed that period when it could have easily been terraformed?

It is just within the habitable range to facilitate this. Terraforming is possible for Mars. It would take great effort, but it is attainable. It is not attainable by humans at the present time, but it is possible for us. Ultimately, it would not be a planet that humans would find very comfortable, but it is possible. It requires creation of a new atmosphere and this would require a greater gravity for such a planet. This can be created by artificial means, but it would not occur naturally.

Materials would need to be transformed to make an atmosphere denser to create conditions for Mars to be habitable. Mars was once, in its early life, a place not too dissimilar to Earth. It did not have the size or mass to support a rich atmosphere, like on Earth. Mars provided the atmospheric protection from ultraviolet rays from your star, thus enabling life to develop more quickly on Earth. Mars lacked the atmosphere to do that. In a sense, Mars was like a child that, in human gestation, did not survive birth.

How does a species overcome its own violent nature?

There is a strong, instinctual, often irrational, confusing desire to survive. Part of this is the natural instinct of all creatures. Often, the creatures will interpret this irrationally as their own sense of protecting themselves. They will often harm others to perpetuate their own life in order to provide for their own needs, feeling that the resources they require to live are limited. There is a sense of confusion, a riot type where there is irrationality, sometimes organized, sometimes only within the individual.

In time, violence is corrected through greater understanding and communication. We also have an instinct within us, a sense of violence. This is suppressed because many life forms have acquired a telepathic sense of a greater social structure, a greater awareness of the interdependence of life in our species and with other species. This creates a sense of understanding where the fear of being deprived because of limited resources is only a concept in the mind. It creates an understanding that violence is not necessary. It is difficult to describe this. It is somewhat foreign to me, even though we understand it, so forgive my ineptness in explaining this.

Yes. I think that it comes down to the belief that there are not enough resources in the Universe, and the fear that they will not get a share.

That is a more precise explanation. It is not physical limitations. It is the expectation or belief that there are limited resources when, actually, there are unlimited means, if the intellect can be applied. As one human of your species once aptly communicated to others of your species: 'The only thing we have to fear is fear itself.' Also, with telepathy, there is a sense of interconnectedness. I believe there is another advanced, but spiritual human term that says, 'One is one's brother's keeper.' That is not just a concept, but also a normal reality within our society because of the telepathic weave of which we are all a part. This comes more naturally for us so the need to act out individually is not necessary. There is a peace and understanding that each is caring and aware of the welfare of others. This makes violence unnecessary. In the evolution of humans this will eventually happen. If you can survive long enough it will. I believe you will and given time, it has already begun.

Yes. Now that I think about it, I have a question on entropy. Does it exist because friction exists or does it stand on its own?

Entropy exists in both means. It exists due to friction in the gradual slowing down, and entropy is also a function of the passage of time. In an initial focal horizon, it begins to slow as time and space spread out. Human beings also, like all life forms, experience entropy. Aging is partly, as we understand it, a symptom of entropy. Many physiological traits of humans can be changed to extend their period of life, as we have, to diminish the effects of entropy. Often, humans, in contact with other species during abductions, have described to us what it means to be old. Initially we did not understand the concept. Now we understand. Often, we leap not only across space, but also across time in our travels. When one is locked on an island in space, left behind, the natural processes of entropy are more self-evident. In traveling across space, time becomes indistinct as part of space travel, as we understand it, across stars and between galaxies. Linear time is an archaic concept and makes a sense of time or aging strange to us. We began to understand by observing humans, and listening to what they were stating. Now we understand fully.

Yes. I can imagine time being able to move in any direction whatsoever. Most people don't think of it that way.

Other

No questions in this session.

Open Session for Comments or Questions

We wish Mary, George, and Steve a fulfilled and rich life. We enjoy their company and presence. We look forward to continued communication. Han is acquainted with George. Others of my species have often had contact with George. Also, in our communication and interaction with Mary, we enjoy her desire to learn and her sense of a higher self that is the basis for all advanced awareness and consciousness about us and other life. She understands and embraces it. We conclude at this time, and I hope that you enjoyed the setting that I provided from my mind to give you a comfortable setting in which we can enjoy our time together. I knew of Mary's love of New Mexico and in my hospitality, I provided that setting. At the same time, I introduced that setting to Steve for his enjoyment. It is with this sense of hospitality that I am pleased that you enjoyed it also. Good night.

Session X, Gravity Waves, Consciousness, Han's World
October 2, 2011

Steve was inducted, given some therapy and then the therapist invited the being known as Han to step forward. The therapist made several adjustments to Steve's vibration and then waited a few minutes for Han to make adjustments.

Steve: In my induction now, in my mind, I am skimming so peacefully and quickly, moving low, over solid clouds. When you change the induction frequency, the image melts the body vibration and it becomes part of space. Our speed accelerates rapidly to a point where space seems to have folded over onto itself. Space folds over and as soon as it does, it unfolds just as quickly. It is as if Han is showing me in my mind how it looks when he travels or leaps across dimensions. It is startling, but there is no impression of traveling instantaneously. We are now near another planet. It is an Earth-looking planet, similar, but different. Han seems to be sharing how their form of space flight looks to them. Before you expect to travel even faster, you are already slowing down. The greatest distance that must be crossed seems to be the briefest part of the whole journey. The planet we are approaching looks like Earth, yet not quite. There are greens and blues, places where you see lights, cities, and clouds. At a distance, I see twin stars, one near, and one smaller or farther away. This is Han's home world.

We are going to ask him to create a space for us to meet. So please give him time to do that.

It is like he is arranging chairs, without chairs, creating a space. This knoll on his planet has strange plants, bright red, like leaves or flowers or something with strange stocks. It is very lovely. There is green grass and he is sitting on a stone. I am reclined on the grass. I have my arm propped up, holding up my head, with my elbow on the ground. Mary is nearby, also comfortable. It seems that this time the setting is on his home planet. The air feels like high altitude. It is thin, but it is comfortable. Breathing is a little more conscious than it normally would be. It feels rather like a sunny fall day on Earth. He says he is ready.

Earth History

Can you tell us what causes cancer in human beings?

It is a manifestation of entropy in its ugliest form. It is one thing that gives humans a sense of dread and fear. It is the accelerated mutation of cells changed by many external environmental sources. Humans have genetic traits that make them susceptible to these sources. This is a physical condition that often occurs in them. It is a complex and varied disease, with many forms of manifestation. It is due to the limitations of humans with their short life spans, some of which can be attributed to this anomaly.

We have also observed that many forms of life experience such diseases in other parts of the Universe. Cancer is not unique to your planet Earth. Many advanced forms of life have conquered this disease and, eventually, so will humans. Many times we have compassionately removed such diseases from individuals because, in the overall plans for contact, these diseases interfere with our work. We eliminate these diseases to compensate.

I have heard of this happening.

We have, in some cases, along with other entities, some of which are of the criminal variety you refer to as greys, made such compensations. Not all greys are criminals. They permeate through our areas of influence, too. Many, by human values, would consider them to be a 'good' species. They, too, have often had compassion and healed their human subjects. This has mutual benefits. It permits these other entities to continue their own experiments. It prevents spoilage of their harvest. Humans are often abducted very early in their life spans when they begin to create mature sexual characteristics consistent with their species.

We found that, due to environmental concerns common to Earth, many entities will abduct humans early in their life period when the samples they seek are less tainted by possible environmental toxins or radiation found on this planet. Thus, they obtain a purer specimen.

What about the actual conditions of the human body? For instance, if the body were a little too alkaline, would that have an effect?

There is what is called a PH range from alkaline to acidic. This is a fundamental understanding in human physiology and the physiology of many life forms. The PH range would astonish most humans in many of the beings that they have yet to discover. The PH levels could be one preexisting condition for the formation of the disease.

What about antioxidants - are they actually helpful?

Antioxidants can help inhibit many of these conditions that we are discussing. They create a more beneficial condition for coping with cancers, but they are not a cure in and of themselves. However, in combination with other treatments, they are very beneficial.

Just for example, if a human being maintained a slightly alkaline state and took a reasonable supply of antioxidants, would this be helpful to them in preventing cancer?

Yes.

I assume that stress is also a factor in bringing on cancer.

The human mind, as well as our own minds and the minds of many sentient creatures, is very much interconnected in ways that humans do not yet fully appreciate, but they are learning quickly, particularly in the half last century. These emotional factors affect the physical body and its health. In human cultures, mental health is as important as physical health. This is often not appreciated.

In many ways, your physical understanding of the human body is commendable, and yet, there is much to look forward to in the knowledge you will soon gain. Mental illness, in many ways, still needs further strides, not so much in its treatment, but in its view in human society. It is seen with some apprehension and distain when, at the same time, humans will show fellow humans compassion when it is a physical ailment. They do not often understand that a physical ailment is also mental. There is this inconsistency we observe. That, in time, may be corrected.

In earlier sessions, I have mentioned about the deviant behavior of some within our species. Some minor deviance is welcome because, from this, new ideas and perspectives can emerge.

Maybe due to their inability to have the community of mind that is possible through telepathy that our species enjoys, humans are limited in their understanding of mental illness or in appreciating its extent within your society. It often does not become apparent to you until such disabilities become violent. Much of mental illness is also confused with anxiety, simply because of the human condition. Anxiety has been a survival instinct for humans. When human anxiety lingers beyond its original instinctive purpose, it causes much self-inflected pain. In our encounters with humans, we often spend a great deal of energy in soothing human minds as they come in contact with our species and many other species. It is difficult to communicate with them when their minds are, in effect, screaming. We talk with them in a calm and positive manner. We understand this anxiety, but it takes time. We are patient. Sometimes some of our own species become annoyed with this, but in many ways, humans are still primitive. Due to their lack of exposure to other species in the Universe, this would be quite understandable.

Is there an effective way that we might use to remove the space junk that is now floating around in our planet?

Yes, there is a way. The level of technology that man is presently using causes this. The energies used in your primitive chemical rockets reflect a relatively inefficient use of energy where a great deal of stored energy is needed to lift a payload into space. Many of your technologies hearken to our early history. Humans will need to minimize their mess, as you call it. We travel inter-dimensionally. This enables us to travel through this orbiting traffic jam. Your space junk is not of consequence to us. Therefore, in communicating with you, I wish to assure you that this is only a problem for humans, not for us. This is just one more commonly observed indication among most evolving species of Earth having reached an early level of technology to move into space.

Thank you for that.

You probably are aware of an individual with the last name of Spielberg. He has directed a number of films that depict interactions with humans and non-Earth beings. Do you know of him?

Yes we do know of him. He is one of several entertainers in human society who has created stories about contacts, some imagined, some not. These stories have created physical wealth. We see these in a sympathetic way as helping my role in opening up broader perspectives of human consciousness about the Universe. These films have created new perspectives and thoughts about aliens, as they imagine seeing us and others like us. These stories show humans a broader understanding and appreciation for other life forms. In reality, it helps humans be more tolerant of differences they see within themselves.

Yes. I see him somewhat as an educator, not so much in facts, but in developing an open mind.

Mr. Spielberg has a unique talent for retaining many of his younger, childlike qualities and perspectives. This has benefited his art and his skills as a communicator and educator. It has also has benefited him in his material wealth.

His ability to understand those who appreciate his work has created great rewards for his skills. His many interests include extraterrestrial contact. He has often provided some of his rewards as an artist by providing the funding for some projects, including the primitive SETI experiment. We keep a close watch on many. It is to our benefit to know this in our interaction with your species.

Zeta Reticuli History

Here on Earth, we keep pets. For me, the pets I keep are more like allies and friends. Do you have those kinds of relationships with other species on your home planet?

You might say that we regard the greys as pets, but in a more sophisticated way. The greys perform many roles. Many of those that you call greys are of wholly organic origins. Some are biomechanical. They perform many functions. They are not servants. They live equally in our social pattern, but we often see them as companions in a larger sense. Humans often have a desire to care for others, and have a love bond for living creatures on their planet. They need to express that affection and to receive affection from pets. Often, in our visits, pets can be troublesome. Many have to be subdued by making them passive to suppress the natural protective instincts they have for their pet owners. We appreciate the loyalty they often express. It is understood. This is part of the human culture to have pets and we accept this. Know that, in our own encounters, your pets are not harmed. They are just rendered passive until we depart. This is to reduce the consequential random elements possible from such contact. When you regard your pets as your allies and friends it creates a positive reflection upon you as a species, even though these 'pets' often only react instinctively.

What do you teach your own children about how to interact with life forms such as plants and trees, as well as less intelligent animals?

In our travels throughout the Universe we have encountered many higher advanced forms of life. Some of these have even attained a spiritual energy level of evolution beyond physical instrumentalities. We regard these with respect. In relationship to that, and how they regard us, we embody that and regard, in turn, other life forms with the same respect. In the broader respect of the Universe and our place in it, whether more advanced or less advanced, we try to regard all life as being precious. We also see it as a physical manifestation of the processes of the Universe where physical matter becomes self-aware and intelligent. Any life form that has the ability to become self-aware is regarded by us as very special. We have learned this by various means from our travels throughout the Universe and regard such with the same respect.

You had mentioned that one aspect of your work is communicating with various species. Could you tell us a little bit about some of your other work? Where do you hope to take your contact with this advanced energy form?

I am in contact with many species. Some contact is on a similar level as our species, some more advanced, and some less advanced. How I communicate with humans is different from how I communicate with the Pleiadians, for example. The wavelength and breadth of communication is more expansive with the Pleiadians. Communication with humans, with no disrespect, is limited only by where you are in your state of evolution. You might become overwhelmed. We must respectfully process it in such a way to provide it at a rate you can absorb, comprehend, and relate back. In many ways, I must use diplomacy, even in our own community of mind. The need is more acute where diplomacy must be used with greater tact in species that does not yet have the ability to communicate telepathically.

Many forms of communication are taken for granted. We are mindful of this. For instance, humans, without telepathy, could easily be prone to misunderstanding any intent and purpose in our contact with humans. Species contact around the Universe is a normal and natural function. At the current level of our contact with humans, you are, by our perspective, quite isolated in your thought about how you regard your place in the Universe. It is with gentle influence or persuasion that we are slowly bringing you into the knowledge of your place in a larger Universe.

Aside from communicating with many species, do you have another job to do?

A job in the context of providing shelter and security?

No. Where you expend your energies to be of service.

We all have our roles to play in the greater context of an interconnected society. There are many roles performed by many others. I perform a function, often in contact with many species, Earth being one of them. I suppose this is my role or 'job.'

Would you describe how your eyes are different from human eyes, particularly in their capabilities?

Our eyes are able to see greater wavelengths of light, and also see frequencies in the non-light frequencies in both the infrared and the ultraviolet. Our eyes are somewhat larger than human eyes. Our eyes are also seen as a pathway for telepathic communication. We often use this in our contact with humans to focus our thoughts in the human mind. We can more easily see in relative darkness than can humans. Our larger eyes gather more light and the other wavelengths. This gives us an advantage in our contacts and discrete exploration of your planet.

This is just one feature of our physical characteristics. Part of this may have been due to our adaptation to space flight. Also, perhaps our early missing link had characteristics we retained that helped it survive in its early evolutionary development. We came from a form of bird-like humanoid being.

Are you able to see developing thought forms and do they come in a large range of colors?

Yes. Some humans call these auras. Certain characteristics and colors prevail in certain creatures. Humans, in particular, have a conspicuous effect, which we often use to assess their emotional state when we are in contact with such humans. They provide a further indication of the emotional energies they randomly radiate. This is unconscious to you, but we can see it quite readily.

Most of us don't see the colors, but we certainly sense someone's emotions when they are nearby, if the emotions are strong enough. We have that condition where hair stands up on the back of our necks or our arms when we feel that something is different.

This is part of an instinctual response, often seen in many such animals, humans being one of them. This is part of the instinctual primitive response often called 'fight or flight,' which we have often seen in our encounters with humans. It is important for us to understand this instinctual response to our encounters, both with our craft and in direct contact. That knowledge enables our contacts with humans to have outcomes that are more positive. It is our way of making adjustments, which must occur in the interaction with many species.

Concerning some of your other senses, say in orders of magnitude or percentage, how is your hearing compared to humans?

Our hearing is not as acute as human hearing. This is the best that we can understand. It is not as important in many ways. Telepathic skills have replaced much of our sense of hearing. Hearing has become less important due to this. We seem now to hear with our minds.

Is that also true of your sense of smell?

Our sense of smell is actually heightened. We have no explanation for this. It could be a distortion of our own perception of ourselves. We know in the case of many humanoids, including humans, the sense of smell has a larger imprint on their memory. It is perhaps with us, too. It is perhaps on an equal level in sensory ability. It may be magnified by memories of those associations that may seem to be embellished, when they are actually not.

Certainly smell is a very evocative sense for us and easily brings back memories.

We do not deny, in our own evolutionary development, that the sense of smell has contributed both as a survival trait, and to our earlier concepts of reproduction. In our covert fieldwork visits here on Earth, we enjoy many fragrances. Many plants and other beings have scents that are part of their normal biological gestations. We enjoy those, too. Scents of flowers are particularly memorable and unique.

When we human beings are paying attention, we enjoy these things, too.

We have noticed this.

Has your sense of touch diminished during your evolution or has it increased?

Certain areas of our anatomy are heightened, particularly our fingers and fingertips. This is due, in part, to our psychotronic abilities in linking with our technologies. Our minds, through thoughts, connect directly with controls in our craft. These have become embellished and heightened and often it is a conduit for controlling some forms of tools that you call technology. These have been heightened out of necessity or practicality. Other parts of our selves have diminished in sensitivity, perhaps in compensating.

Is clothing a rather normal thing for humanoids to wear, aside from our planet? Is clothing a part of your society?

In our society we permit a certain sense of individual vanity to express itself, even though many feel connected in a larger sense, a part of the community of minds. We do not have the sense of modesty that we have noticed in humans. We are comfortable wearing clothes, as you call them, garments. Many garments that we wear, particularly in contact with humans, are not merely clothing, but also protection from biological contamination between both humans and entities. There is a psychotronic magnification of some entities' organic sensory abilities through this 'clothing.' This provides enhanced awareness around them for their own safety and provides an early warning. Clothing can, we admit, be a form of fashion, but clothing provides a serious function in many types of situations.

Spirituality

What causes species, when they die, to leave imprints in material objects that play back sometimes? I am speaking particularly of what we might call 'haunting' where there is no consciousness involved, but the sound plays back. How is it imprinted and how is it released?

In your question about our eyes, I remarked about our many abilities to sense certain energies that are radiated by humans. Some are a physical manifestation. Some are energies that transcend the physical. Sometimes a wake or imprint can be left behind on many physical objects. This residual energy lingers sometimes for a short time.

I believe those energies are the ones to which I am referring. Is it strong emotion that causes them to imprint, and why do they imprint at one time, but not at other times?

There is a kind of energy frequency that is radiated by humans and all life forms that leave a shadow or wake of residual energy behind them. Often, these energies also appear to our eyes as certain colors. We can often tell by the person who left these residues what their physical and emotional state was at that time. Many of the encounters we have with humans are during times when they are coping with great emotional stress, such as a loss or big change in their relationship with others in their social units.

We respond out of curiosity. We can use these energies, which humans unconsciously project, to gauge their own life's sense of wellness or stress. Some ghosts are an amplified residue of their past energies, perhaps made so in the transition from physical life to the afterlife. It is the resonance of all life forms throughout the Universe. It is a part of a larger energy that encompasses and envelops all life forms.

Since every life form emits its own kind of energy when it passes over, what is to stop all those energies from absorbing into materials and then coming back and creating incredible chaos?

This is a mystery to us. Is it perhaps that each life energy is both a wave and particle, emitting a certain identity or uniqueness while, at the same time, amalgamating into a larger whole? This is a primitive residue apparent in our telepathic community of mind. It does challenge our own species' view about a sense of social identity. Perhaps this is an evolutionary throwback to an earlier time before the ability to communicate telepathically existed.

It is really difficult for us to tell, but this phenomenon seems to be tied to wood in old houses, among other materials, and also to stone structures. I don't know that I have heard of this playback phenomenon out in the woods.

Wood is an organic structure.

I guess that stone might have some quartz in it that might magnify sound, but I am only guessing.

There are certain energies, even within stones, with a different frequency, that harkens back even to the creation of the Universe. Part of all matter that exists within its nuclear resonance has a type of echo from the original creation of the Universe.

Contact

Han, are you familiar with an individual whose name was John Mack? He was a psychiatrist. I believe he was attached to Harvard University.

Yes, I know of John Mack. He is in the thoughts we downloaded from humans, in our contacts with humans. There are impressions of this gentleman, either from direct contact or from humans reading about him. We are aware of him and we are aware of his spirit. His spirit still exists in the Universe.

Yes. I met him and his work helped to guide me to open up to this kind of communication. He seemed to be very compassionate, and I appreciate who he was and who he is in spirit.

There have been a number of very large triangles seen in the sky near Grass Valley. Are you familiar with that?

These are part of a continuing exercise. Some species require genetic material of humans. They are part of the illegal, criminal activity that is often associated with these beings. The craft themselves are not improper, but the creatures that use them behave improperly. Triangles, as you call them, due to their shape, are interstellar and interdimensional craft, which use shifts in dimensional frequencies to conceal their presence. They appear quite large by human standards and indiscrete, but they have the ability to conceal themselves just as well as our craft. The size, for their function, is rather inconsequential. There has been activity in many areas. Placerville, for instance, is just one in that general area. Many contacts are being continued and maintained in the normal process that has been going on for some time.

Yes. May I ask you about one of the cases I have been working on in that area?

Yes.

There is the case of Lenore (pseudonym) and her brother who have seen one of these crafts. Lenore, we believe, has been taken intermittently.

She has.

Do you think her brother may also have been taken?

No. Not at this time.

What about her mother?

Yes. It is the females in this social unit that are of interest at this time.

Does it go further back in lineage?

Yes. Also, including in some males.

Can you tell me how many generations back?

Three generations. It is an experiment. There is a particular genetic lineage that this social unit possesses that is of interest. Also, in return, in gratitude for their *unwilling* service, many of these species have provided physical cures for ailments for these humans, such as cancer, as we discussed earlier. This is part of maintaining the integrity of the genetic experiment being conducted.

Has Lenore or her mother ever had cancer?

Lenore has. Her Mother has not. Lenore's father had cancer.

Chapter Two: Alien Biology and Consciousness

Do you happen to know what part of her body was affected?

In Lenore's case it was some of her lymphatic system.

And her father?

I do not have that information.

Steve would like to ask about an incident in his childhood in which he felt he was interacting with some kind of an alien being who was quite friendly to him and almost paternal. Do you have any knowledge of that incident?

I will refer to a number of others of my species in the interconnected weave that we have. We recall contact with him early in his physical life. He seemed to be more receptive than most. We apologize if some of these telepathic contacts and physical contacts were, in some way, distressing to him. This often occurs with many we encounter that I spoke of earlier. We sensed a feeling of warmth, a feeling of familiarity from him. We have an image of holding his hand and guiding him through a lonely period, but a wonderful period, too. He had a wonderful childhood in which he was loved and felt secure. He often felt uncomfortable in school in not knowing how to fit in. Many humans encounter this in their emotional and social development. This is only natural. Our species also learned this at a very early age. It is part of growth.

During that time period in his childhood, was there something that happened in the house next door that was unusual?

There were several visits. One such visit occurred in his parent's backyard when we showed him our craft, primarily a form of energy, which was quite daunting, astonishing, and frightening for a young mind. Several times we implanted false memories, concealing these visits. One such implanted memory was unfortunate, but effective, thus creating a nightmare of a situation based on much human religious mythology, which we often exploit. Another was a visit by us where we introduced the children of our species. We masked the memory of this visit by planting in his mind a memory of visiting the neighbors next door. This is not actually what occurred. It was a visit by our species, but we felt that implanting this memory of visiting his neighbors concealed our visit.

We planted the idea in his mind that he did. There was no trauma in this particular visit. We actually introduced some of our younger, what humans would regard as alien children, to play with him. We wished to study his interactions and we must say that he was very promising and happy with these children of ours. It showed promise for future contacts.

It is not a surprise that Steve is here today, being used for communication between us. This role as a communicator began when we discovered this faculty in him in that meeting with our offspring. He has certain fundamental qualities that all life has. He sees past certain prejudices that humans may foster and sees beyond certain appearances and mannerisms that would be strange to others. He is accepting and comfortable with them so it is not surprising that he has a longing to investigate many (reports of) craft and also any false reports that are of human origins. It is his unconscious desire to connect with us.

The Universe

I have always felt that travel was the best educator.

Yes. There are such wonders for humans yet to discover out there. There are wonders in learning about us and many other species. This will be of benefit to humans in helping them determine what they are and what they will become. Their identities will not diminish. As they gain a broader sense of their place in the Universe, it will embellish and enrich all that they know.

Other

No questions in this session.

Open Session for Comments or Questions

Is there any final thing you would like to say to us today?

The human mind has great capacity. You are capable of such great dreams and nightmares. Part of this is a manifestation of your evolution. In the individual lives that make up your species, know that there is a higher good, beyond all of us, that each species eventually realizes. Throughout the Universe, each species shares a first question, which universally remains the ultimate last question.

Until we talk again, thank you very much.

Session XI, Malone Family, Implants, Serpo, Echos
October 8, 2011

Steve was inducted and given some therapy. The therapist invited the being known as Han to step forward. After a long silent pause, the therapist adjusted Steve's vibration and then waited a few minutes for Han to make adjustments. Then another invitation was extended.

We invite Han to meet your vibration and to work with us. Steve, go ahead and describe what you see.

Steve: I see forest. The air is filled with insects and Han has somehow created a means to hold them back from him and from us. I think we are in Russia in the Tunguska area. It is isolated. I think he likes it because of the astronomical event that occurred here. We are sitting in a meadow and the ground is curiously soft, like a thick carpet. The ground moss creates a soft mat that gives slightly under your feet. The three of us are together in a kind of triangle of three, or perhaps four. There might be another entity somewhere in the distance. There are trees and intensely blue skies with huge, fluffy clouds. It is summertime.

Is there water nearby?

Oh, not a river, but a sense of water everywhere, in the ground, in marches. Yes, now I see a very active stream at a distance, like from a spring melt. It is warm, but not unpleasant. It could be as if we were camping, but it is in an area where there is a lot of new growth. You can also see trees knocked down by the blast from the event in 1908, the explosion in the sky. The trees have all fallen the same way as far as the eye can see. Only the old trees are the ones that are down. There are new trees and fresh vibrant growth and vitality. It is the middle of nowhere, but we feel safe.

It is a wonderful example of destruction and rebirth. I am speaking now to Han. If he is available, please ask him to step forward.

Steve: He is here and he looks forward to talking with Mary.

Earth History

Han, you have selected this place that we both know about. Scientists are telling us that it was probably a meteorite conglomeration enclosed in a comet-like covering of ice that exploded above the ground. Is this correct or was it something else?

I chose this place to show the renewal of life, an example of how humans can also change. This place shows Earth's great ability to regenerate itself. From this destruction comes new life and new possibilities. Also, I chose it because it is isolated and we will not be disturbed. Your scientists are correct. It was an extinct comet about 100 meters wide. Though extinct, it still contained considerable frozen water, with its remaining stony core, permitting penetration into this planet's lower atmosphere. These comet elements violently exploded when it entered this planet's atmosphere. This is not uncommon on planets with little or no atmosphere and many craters. This one could have been a cataclysmic event, but it was not.

Is that because it exploded above the Earth instead of impacting it with full force?

Yes. This is correct. This is not unusual for the conditions present, a thick atmosphere combined with the right proportional mass of water and stony material. Some come through with most of their physical properties still intact, surviving the atmosphere. This one obviously exploded and scattered in a wide area. Eventually, Earth scientists and their many theories developed an accurate conclusion. It was a comet-like object that approached the Earth. It had some elements of ice, but it was predominately of rock. If it were a full-fledged comet it would have likely been noticed before its final approach. There are thousands of these orbiting objects in your planetary system.

We were wondering what you could tell us about hummingbirds, in particular, whether they originated on this planet or are from somewhere else?

There is a combination of both. They originated on Earth, and some, due to planetary conditions, were transported to other planets to complement their existing ecology. Often, these birds, as a species, will diminish in numbers. Sometimes extraterrestrial adaptations are re-transplanted back to originating sources to enrich the species again.

We are so glad to hear that because it is one species we really enjoy having around.

They do exist elsewhere and are sometimes reintroduced here to reinvigorate the genetic strain and to increase their population numbers here and elsewhere. They have an important role to perform in the pollination of plants and in the spreading of spores to increase plant growth. Reciprocally, the plants provide sugars for these animals in a symbiotic relationship.

Are you aware of the illness that has befallen many of the bats?

We have noticed this to some degree. We are more concerned with the mass extinction of the insects you refer to as bees. They seem to be dying at a sudden rate. Part of this is the natural restarting of life. Perhaps the reason why we are in this setting is to note this restarting of life. However, the Earth is changing and insects are often the early indicators of these changes. It is of concern to us and it should be a concern to humans, too, especially in how their habitat is changing form, due to climate and the human influence on its environment. It occurs in ways that often go unnoticed by many.

Many of us are concerned, but there seems to be differing opinions as to the cause of their decline. Do you have any idea what some of the major factors are?

Some of them are genetic strains that have weakened their genetic strength through overpopulation and now require infusion of genetic material to invigorate their species. This is partly due to the way insects reproduce so quickly. Predominately, it is due to environmental changes in temperature and in the use of chemicals in controlling so-called pests to subordinate the species to allow humans to grow their food. These insects are also accidentally sprayed.

Are these new chemicals, from the last ten years?

Yes.

Let's hope the manufacturers take responsibility and figure that out quickly.

Often, in the urgency of farmers to create a cure for certain pests, they did not foresee other consequences that were not intended. Soon they will have to be adapted if their continued harvest, of which insects such as bees are an essential part, is to be sustained.

Zeta Reticuli History

Is your species able to create heavy metals?

Atomic elements?

I am referring to the heavy metals, such as gold or platinum. Do they have to be found?

They can be created. We now have abilities that humans do not have available. To create these artificially, certain heavy elements are created naturally, particularly from neutron sources of energy. Certain neutron stars are great factories for many heavy elements. Your planetary system or solar system is quite abundant in many heavy elements. Part of this is due to their original creation from neutron sources.

Steve was looking at some pictures of a bat and it struck him how similar the structure was to your arm and hand structure. He could see that clearly.

The images that I have in mind that I see in Steve's mind are not dissimilar. They are very familiar to us. Our hands and joints, originating from flying beings, are not an accident. They are familiar and similar to birds or your bat mammals. The bat is a remarkable species on your planet. We could almost rename the planet the 'bat planet' for its amazing population of these creatures that inhabit and provide an important part of the planet's ecology. They project a form of radar impulse for navigation. This provides a means to catch their food and navigate in darkness. They also use it to communicate with each other. In a way, it reminds of us that we use a similar form of *echoing* our communication, a resonating energy that we use to communicate with our species.

Spirituality

No questions in this session.

Contact

(The following questions stem from an interview with the Robert Malone family covering the experiences of the father, mother, and child, Nancy. These events occurred during World War II and continue to the present day with the daughter.)

Concerning a case that we had, the Malone case, that involved Nancy's mother and particularly her father in the military, can you fill us in a little bit on that case regarding an event in Germany involving a train?

Due to the World War II conflict, toward the end, many entities visited the Earth, studying you and your behavior. We could see the great political struggles that were encompassing your planet worldwide, touching all who lived on this planet. A great choice was being violently decided, the choice of which road your human history would follow. We are pleased with the result. By human terms, a dark age would have fallen if Germany and Japan prevailed, subjugating one human life for another. There were those who thought they were superior when they were not. We have seen such things throughout the Universe. It was of great importance to us to study this struggle. Many of the objects that you called 'foo fighters' were intelligent forms of energy. They could be referred to as 'probes.' Some were occupied to enable close range observation of the many curious human activities with their primitive technology. The Malone family was part of this. The husband and father in this family was Robert Malone. His military activity was to secretly study reports of our activities. Our activities did not go unnoticed by humans in your military. In human culture, the military is to provide safeguards against an unknown. Their reaction to our craft is understandable.

We noticed that Robert Malone was often in places where he encountered our species and other species. He, in many ways, was a hopeful, positive sign that one day, a deeper contact and relationship would be possible between humans, our species, and other species. We noticed that they did not wish to harm us. Sometimes they would try to sequester us away from others on your planet during our explorations of your planet. In part, this was due to their concepts, which we share, that initial contact should be done carefully, in a discrete fashion. Often, the Army would try to keep us away, more for our own protection. They would often retrieve our beings, our scouts. The Army confined them, but our abilities made this confinement comical.

Was there any loss of alien life during a train derailment near a tunnel during World War II?

In southern Europe, a train derailed, causing damage and loss of life. Many of these passengers were refugees and were in the process of being returned to their former homes. It is where the Malones had met. They already had a relationship. During this time, our craft appeared, frightening many of the passengers on the train. This was in an isolated area. We were observing this activity to see if these humans were being transported to the concentration camps. We learned, in time, that they were not, but were being returned back to their homelands. With that knowledge, we withdrew from the scene of the accident.

So, the Malones, when they said they saw bodies, they were not alien bodies, but refugees? Is that correct?

There were refugees, many of whom were sickly and malnourished. At other times, alien bodies of our species and others were found in other locations that the Malones were involved with, particularly Robert Malone.

Concerning Robert Malone, his wife said she took him to a hospital when he became ill. He wasn't very ill and he seemed to disappear. I believe they told her that he died in the hospital and they refused to produce his body. She believes that is not the case because she thinks she saw him afterwards. Do you have any knowledge about what happened to Robert Malone?

In the unusual behavior resulting from interacting and maintaining the secret of our species' contact with humans, many curious circumstances developed, which we do not understand. This behavior of secrecy is foreign to us. We understand it, but we see a comedy/tragedy, to use a human term, in the desire to know and yet, at the same time, a desire to keep secret certain situations. Robert Malone was a pawn in this. The Army created the deception that he had died, to the great pain of his family unit. He later died a natural death, not long after. It seemed so unnecessary and so fruitless to stage this deception. It is part of the human condition that occurs when humans decide what knowledge should be withheld from others of your species, like the Serpo Project.

In the Serpo Project, we returned many humans who wished to return to Earth, yet the humans who were returned were sequestered away from other humans because of the knowledge they had acquired about us. They were not permitted to share among other humans the knowledge of our culture. This is frustrating to us. We do not fully understand. They were not permitted to speak of their experiences with our species. Many of the Serpo humans requested to be returned and were returned to our planet. The Serpo humans who remained on Earth, like the Malones, had to live alone in their secret, isolated.

I think that Nancy may still be in contact, in some way, with other species.

Yes, she is.

She is of a special genetic origin in that she was not created biologically in the normal fashion. She was a product of scientific manipulation by humans in that she was an early product of genetic engineering by the Army. Her father had certain physical characteristics of his age and was unable to create offspring in the normal fashion. His sperm was collected and inserted into the female who was Nancy's mother. This was done artificially as an experiment by the Army. This is partly why Nancy is of interest to us and to others. She experiences continued visits as a result. She is considered a legacy of Robert Malone, a product of his genetic background. Robert is considered by our species to be an ally and friend. Robert's and his family's sacrifices did not go unnoticed by us. In the early contacts with our species he acted in a very positive and humane way toward our species. Robert represented humanity well in his difficult situation and with his responsibilities as a military officer. His abilities and instinctual desires as a human being were of note. He showed kindness and cared for our species when some of our species were temporarily marooned on this planet. Our species remembers Robert Malone, in particular, for his kindness, bravery, and his courage to face the unknown in a noble and just way.

Yes, I had some sense of what incredible pressures he must have been under and yet, he seemed to have maintained his sense of right and wrong.

He was abducted. We know of his clear sense of right and wrong and the turmoil he experienced. We know that his purpose, in a larger perspective, was a good one in following his government's instructions.

He was abducted before he was in the Army?

No. He was abducted when he was in the Army. When he was interacting with our species he would sometimes be abducted, along with his wife and child. They were of interest to us, and we needed the knowledge about others of our species who were returned and others who did not survive. We needed to read their minds (the Malones) and memories to understand what was occurring beyond the normal telepathic connection that we feel with our species when they are away from us. The Malones felt much like the aliens they encountered, having a sense of purpose and mission and, at the same time, a terrible sense of aloneness.

A sense of aloneness?

Alone, trapped by their secret.

Steve would like to know if 'screened memories' will continue to be used and required in abduction cases or if this will eventually fall away as people become fully aware of the reality of visitors.

The individual human is fairly benign, curious, and has certain emotional frailties. People in a group act differently, irrationally, without telepathy or a community of mind. Each creates a fear of uncertainty about what the individual may be able to handle that a group cannot handle. In observing this, we have been able to create certain screened memories, often used to conceal our true activities. Other times, pleasant memories are planted to conceal certain unhappiness that we often encounter in abductees. This is done not to deceive. Rather, it is often done as an act of kindness.

Understanding the human condition as emotional responses in the conscious and subconscious minds, and the spirit beyond this that encompasses the soul, we have observed that all of this is joined. Often, we create screened memories because our interactions would be too disruptive to their current life. Our reality and your reality are often different. This is an ongoing process and, in time, you will notice that we have been abducting for many Earth generations. You will notice that a gradual awareness is growing in the general Earth population. There is a lifting of the veil to the reality of our presence here. It is a conditioning process. Still, for many abductees, other species have conducted themselves in a manner considered unethical and improper.

Sometimes, I encounter very strong blocks in clients during hypnotherapy sessions. I see these blocks as a necessary thing for them for their psychological comfort and I will often not push beyond that simply because I know the trauma that may result. Some people really want to know what has happened to them so the process that I use is to unveil memories very gradually. This gradual process eases them into accepting what they see.

You will recall that initially, in my contacts with Steve, I was cloaked in only minimal light in his mind first. Gradually we allowed each of us to become accustomed to each other. We, too, have to grow accustomed to your appearance. It is not unpleasant. In our many travels we have become accustomed to this, but you do not have the benefit of this and we understand. It is with such consideration that we try to ease the human mind to adjust.

Well, I think that taking it very gradually is a good practice.

We understand in your work the skills you possess. This is often taken into account in the process of human contact with an alien species. You are actually integrated into the total contact process. Your role as a healer, a comforter and as one seeking knowledge about us is all accounted for in the whole process. It is with respect that you can see clearer than many do. We feel that it is unfortunate for those who have been hurt by aliens for their own more selfish purposes. Some aliens do not regard forms of life with the same view that they regard themselves. Sometimes we have abducted humans, too, but not for purpose of taking from them, but rather to give them something. Often, this is knowledge, or visions, or a new perspective placed in the mind, including many new ideas and thoughts. One example of this is making you aware of your planet's environment. It has been a continuing process to create awareness. This has been part of the message that we have been giving for some time among several generations of humans. This continues to this day.

For those who are aware that they are being abducted against their wills and experimented upon, not just once, but numerous times, I don't really know what to say to them to help to ease them through the process because I do not believe that it can be stopped. Do you have any suggestions?

The trauma that sometimes comes consciously apparent is often the reason for creating these screened memories, but this is only a partial solution. The subconscious still retains many of the memories. As you know, this is where some of the unpleasant memories still exist as clearly as the conscious memories. Unfortunately, these often these cannot be erased.

The only thing I know to tell them is to look at all their experiences and see that they are being returned to their homes and their families intact.

Unfortunately, some humans have died. Part of it is the emotional shock. Some deaths are deliberate, due to mutilations. These are rare, but they do occur and this is why our species often, without human awareness, work out of your view to enforce laws that many of our species have accepted as the proper means of making contact. Most contacts provide knowledge, and this is as it should be. These contacts should be for exchange, not to take or steal. In our culture, stealing is a selfish act that is not necessary in the framework of our telepathic community. We often borrow and return, but we rarely take away permanently. If we do, we give them something in exchange. Abduction activity (keeping sentient beings permanently without agreement or recompense) is considered illegal.

Concerning the Serpo Project and the planet that our species was taken to in exchange, what is the temperature and humidity there as compared to here?

It has a similar climate in temperature, atmospheric pressure, humidity, and protection from ultraviolet radiation harm to our species and your species, too. It would be considered a warmer planet, but not out of the range of human concepts of weather. It is well within the human range for comfort and an environment that would enable your species to survive or thrive. It is a warm planet, with dryer humidity, similar to a spring desert climate in California, not too hot, but sometimes with very cold temperatures at night.

I am sure your shelters take care of that.

Our shelters provide an adjustment for this. In our hospitality, these shelters have been provided for the human travelers, too, as we would expect our travelers to Earth would be given the same hospitality. All this has been provided for them. Whether it is a temporary or a permanent visit, they have the freewill to live permanently on our planet or to return to Earth.

I hope you found some Serpo exchange adventurers who have been willing to make the choice to remain permanently with you.

Some have found, in comparing their memories of Earth, many things about the environment of our planet and their interaction with our species to be quite pleasant. Perhaps some humans have found our planet more to their liking. There is no war. There is an abundance of food and diversity of life. They become telepathic and begin to have insights connecting into our society. There is no deception or lies. There is an honesty and simplicity that provides them with an atmosphere to explore new things. Even when they see a double shadow from our two suns, as they stand in the desert of our planet, they see a new perspective and a strange new beginning. For many of them there is a sense of adventure they find very appealing. It is not a place that they long to leave and return home. They might define it as a garden by their standards. It is strange new world, not unpleasant. They find, compared to living in Earth's society, what they might consider a happier place, free of crime, hunger, illness and filled with abundance. We are not perfect, but we offer a setting that we hope they find comfortable. It is part of our nature to provide and to be good hosts. As strange as our appearance may be, we understand the need for humans to connect with their own species. They know there are others like them, if they choose to be with only humans to form relationships, to reproduce and to live and die.

When humans are not stressed with having to earn a living and having to deal with violence and governmental problems, I think they would tend to spend their time learning and then sharing that knowledge. Your planet sounds like a much better place for those who would like to learn and share.

You have formed parks for recreation where you often go to clear your minds, what you call vacations. It is a frame of mind. It is like your 'Disneyland,' where you have no concerns. They can return to a simpler life, childlike and yet, very adult at the same time. The importance of work is balanced by an equal need for play. In your species we have learned that this is important. Our species have accommodated for this in the lives of our Serpo guests.

Even our allies, our dogs and cats, know the concept of work and play.

Chapter Three: Earth Has a Protector

The Universe

We were wondering about body form in that a number of species have evolved to be bipedal. Is there a tendency for evolution to move species into the humanoid form for some specific purpose?

It is a form that is very efficient for many tasks, particularly in the creation of tools. From this comes technology and, in turn, the ability to travel between planets. This is not an accident. The human species tended to originate from primates, which is also a humanoid form. Our species originated from a primitive humanoid bird creature and this was our path for evolution. The bird characteristics remain in subtle ways, showing our origin, but our ability to fly by organic means was lost. We have since replaced that with technology.

Stars, i.e., Betelgeuse, if they go supernova, will this affect your species?

If such an occurrence were to happen, it could affect some of the outskirts of our species in those areas of stars. Fortunately, we are spread across a vast distance in which diversification of life has made the possibility of a total loss of our species more difficult. In addition, these stars are monitored. Some go nova. Some go supernova. Should they explode, we can foresee certain conditions arriving at that event horizon. This can be seen early, in time for us to migrate to areas of safety, to other planets and other star systems.

So there would be sufficient time, then, to make arrangements?

Yes. Often, the end of a star's life can be anticipated in time. Indicators, such as an accelerating imbalance between fuel and gravity, in the right conditions, will create an explosion that would destroy not only the star, but also the entire orbiting system for a great distance out. Many of these stars, when they explode, will provide indications and evidence of what you call dark matter and dark energy. They will provide evidence for your continuing knowledge. With the potential of loss of life, we sometimes have to migrate away. We have the ability to do this. We use energies that would be impossible for humans to use at this time, but this is not impossible for us. It is part of the larger community of mind that provides the ability to travel like this. We can move whole populations to safer areas, well in advance of disaster.

I would certainly expect this ability from a species such as yours that has been around for such a long time. Speaking of time, why don't events sometimes run in reverse? What is there about time that prevents events from running in reverse?

Some elements in the Universe accelerate or exist at higher than light speeds. The speed of light was not always the same speed that it is now. In the early Universe, the speed of light was actually faster. One property of the speed of light is the transmutation of time, forwards or backwards. We often see this phenomenon in our travels during the folding of gravity and dark matter into itself, as we use it to hop instantaneously from one galaxy to another. The human notion of, 'Why would aliens visit Earth?' is an amusing and rhetorical question, if they actually pondered it further. The more reasonable question is, 'Why would we not visit?' The ways in which we are able to travel facilitate this. In time effects, one can go backwards, though this is rare, and we are aware of the many paradoxes that could form from this. In order not to change certain time pathways that are connected in many ways, beyond our own comprehension, we approach with care. There are certain things best left well alone.

Yes. I could imagine some of the many paradoxes and that those would increase as one moves along the evolutionary path.

Time is an interconnective weave with many causes and effects along a linear timeline. It is best, as we value and judge certain realities, to view such time distortions as not good or bad. They are just different, but our sense of reality as a species would invariably also be linked to it. Because time distortions expanded across the Universe, affecting many interconnective timelines, these are best left as they are.

When we humans think of time, we think that, as a function of time, everything changes.

Is there anything that remains the same, that is unaffected by time? I am speaking at the most elemental levels.

All physical manifestations are subject to entropy. Many energies renew themselves. Some are very long term and have lasting properties. Others are much shorter in terms of life span. We have used containerized light, which can be used for our libraries to store knowledge in a method that might be difficult for you to grasp at this time. We know that certain properties of the Universe last a long time and we use these properties to attach something we wish to hold and preserve for a long time. Many of the smallest fundamental elements of the Universe, dark matter and atomic structures, last the longest. We notice that in observing the largest things to the very smallest of things, in one form or another, smaller structures last the longest. In a way, they are interconnected to what makes one the other. We feel, as does your species, we are standing in infinity between the most small and most large, as we attempt to comprehend the Universe. I hope that my answer is not too fractured.

No. My thought was that the activity inside of an atom might be the one that lasted the longest.

It is.

I observed, as a child, the echo (repetition) of the spiral.

Echo is a beautiful term, like music, that expresses the resonance that permeates everything in the Universe and touches all beings in life.

Do you think the term 'celestial music' came from that observation? Rather, I meant, 'music of the spheres?'

It is a music that tries, as we understand it, to create an energy, or a feeling at its most fundamental level, akin to an artist's desire to touch the soul so that they know that their expression is touching others in the utmost way that they can conceive in their art. Such music, as artists try to create, touches others in such a fashion.

Would you please describe to us what happens to matter when it is pulled into a black hole and then exits?

There is an inverse response or reaction in those tremendous gravitational forces. There are certain effects that you have yet to observe and learn about which you will find very exciting when you do discover them. It will provide added insights into the interconnectivity between dimensions and other universes. There will be insights that our Universe, through these black holes, or large powerful gravitational anomalies, will provide doorways and touch other universes beyond, what you might refer to as, 'on the other side.' These processes provide doorways to other universes and other dimensions. They are part of a larger view of the astronomy or reality of what we understand in physics.

In your travels, have you seen the other side of a black hole, as material exits the black hole?

In a way, the entire Universe that we know is such matter. It is the issuing forth of matter from dark black holes from other universes. It is matter that has collapsed and has formed in our Universe. In a way, all that we are, ourselves, are of such matter. It is through this passage way that matter disappears elsewhere and reappears somewhere else. We are the product of black holes and other universes.

I had never thought of it, but I can certainly envision that.

What is death, but just a transition into another form, much like its old form in its most fundamental elements? In a way, like our setting here today in Tunguska, we are in the middle of death and rebirth. In our reality, the black hole is considered something ominous because it would discontinue our current existence, but it would only be transmuted into a new existence somewhere else, where our consciousness would have to take another pathway to transcend. This physical transformation would be a separate path from our current spiritual path. We would have to rejoin on the other side and, ultimately, would have to reconnect in some form.

These are very nebulous or profound concepts, but it is what we have seen and observed in various ways on our travels. It is also what we have learned from other explorers. We share our knowledge with many physical and spiritual beings. We are all asking the same questions.

I would think that we might need to step aside so that other life forms can have space to begin life and have experiences.

It is not one life form displacing another. It is just the natural evolution of the Universe itself, folding in on itself and then re-emerging again.

Speaking of that process, what is the source of the process of evolution?

Evolution is the interaction of different elements, different life, and different species. There is a need to adapt to survive or to create new forms for survival in the natural instinct to survive. To do better than the other species, each species competes with other life forms. This creates the engine for evolution.

My next question concerns Hubble. As we peer into the far edges of the Universe, the speed of light and the great distances confound what we are able to gather. We are not able to get a true, current picture of the edge of our Universe. If we could see the edge of the Universe as it really exists now, what would we see?

The Hubble is, for humans, a significant accomplishment that humans have desired to achieve for some time. Hubble has provided a window for you into the galaxy that we already see. We express and share the joy in the knowledge that you are learning through this amazing, but relatively primitive instrument. Still, it is one of great advancement for humans. There are other observatories being built and placed in Earth orbit that will provide even deeper views back in time, literally to the theoretical point of origin of the Universe. You will notice a rapid blossoming of matter. Your scientists will notice that light moved even faster in the first few minutes and seconds of the birth of the Universe. You will notice manifestations that will challenge your current views of how the Universe began. Some of these beginnings we have hinted to you. (This refers to the colliding of membranes of universes.) However, there are other discoveries we wish you to have the pleasure of learning about for yourselves. Knowing the human condition, the best is yet to come and with more advanced instruments, your species will be able to look farther back in time. You will see wonders that will change your views of matter, energy, and light.

We will see those things, but what we will be seeing would have happened a very long time ago. How can we ever know what is happening now at the edge of the Universe?

The edge, due to dark matter, is accelerating at an ever-increasing rate. Stars may one day disappear. It is hard to imagine, even for our species, a time when the sky will be black, without stars, without destinations. We were like you in your primitive ships when you used a star to sail by. We also know that concept. In our way, we still navigate by the stars. It is a longing for and an enjoyment that, as a seafaring species, we share in what we see in the sky. Your species and ours are both star farers. It would be with great sadness when the time should come that the Universe would accelerate at a rate where the stars begin to break into different pieces. This is part of a process that, in quantum physics, will ultimately complete a cycle. This cycle will create a new Universe. This surpasses even our vast, but limited understanding. We are still pondering these mysteries, and as such, we look to the future with awe and trepidation, as all species do, including humans. In our adaptation, we have learned that we can adjust to many things. We love to travel and visit other places or planets. This is permitted by the abundant energies around us, free for travel and exploration. This touches our souls in a very deep way. We see, in humans, in their primitive ships, how you, too, navigate by the stars. It is with this affection that we share our celestial travel. In that, we can identify with you.

That is a very beautiful way to compare.

Other

No questions in this session.

Open Session for Comments or Questions

Steve is going through emotional distress with these memories of the suffering of the Malones. He needs to know that these are just temporary. It is part of my feelings that I am expressing to you Mary, through him. He is having difficulty with these memories.

Yes. He is taking on the emotion of aloneness.

I am sorry for this. He will be fine. It is only temporary. It is what needs to be communicated to you, and he has done this well for this purpose.

Thank you. I will help Steve with that. Then, until we meet again.

I am glad you enjoyed the setting of renewal. Life continues and so will our meetings.

Session XII, GMFs, Disease, J-Rod, Bob Lazar, S-4
October 17, 2011

Steve was inducted. The therapist invited the being known as Han to step forward. Therapist made several adjustments to Steve's vibration and then waited a few minutes for Han to make adjustments.

We invite Han to meet your vibration and to work with us. Steve, go ahead and describe what you see.

Steve: I see curved walls, smooth ceilings, and smooth floors. It seems to be some kind of craft.

(Han has provided a glimpse of a craft due to Steve's curiosity about what they look like inside. With that expressed, Han says he is ready for questions.)

Earth History

I would like to talk to you about a place in Siberia. The place is called Akushka. The natives call it the Valley of Death because people who go into this valley become quite ill, especially with skin conditions. In addition, there are huge metal 'cauldrons,' approximately 30 feet across. There is folklore or mythology about an epic battle, with fireballs shooting up into the sky and the forest turning upside down. Some of these half spheres or metal cauldrons seem to be turned upside down with some kind of support system. There were bright balls that would shoot out of the top of these structures. Are you familiar with that area or any of it history?

Akushka has many mysterious dwellings that have secret passageways into these structures, just under the ground. They are from earlier cultures that dwelled there. There are also places where the former Soviet Union exploded many atomic devices. The Soviets, to demonstrate their political prowess, irresponsibly detonated some very large devices. Technologically, these irresponsible acts left many areas with harmful radiation that have not been discussed very much.

Because the Siberian area of your Earth is relatively low in population, these matters have not come to the forefront in discussions, but fallout exists there. These are often the sources of these 'valleys of death.' They create an environment that is toxic to life, to humans in particular. These areas are away from the initial areas of explosions, but have moved, due to winds, and deposited forms of radiation downwind of these earlier detonations. The large explosions not only sent accumulative amounts of radioactive fallout around the planet, but as a result, many local areas also suffered. These are the origins of some of these local cultural myths. The primitive people who live there are unaware of the dangers. These are not healthy places by human standards. Other nations have similar areas, but Akushka is most acute.

In that case, it is just as well that they have myths that keep them out of the valley.

The myths serve a good purpose in warning and keeping people away for their own health. We have not illuminated much further because the psychology is sufficient to fulfill its purpose.

Question from 'Doc,' a medical doctor:

Doc: What are we doing as humans (eating, other activities) that is detrimental to having much longer lives?

Population is the major problem. Overpopulation causes food scarcity. Disease becomes more prevalent in dense populations. Resources, food, medicine, fresh air and clean water, become strained, promoting hunger and disease. Major stress prolongs itself when resources are strained. Particularly in the context of overpopulation, food is often manufactured to greatly extend the supply of food beyond what a planet can normally grow and sustain. With these extended growing practices and the creation of certain processed foods, foods are created that are not as good as organic. However, certain organic foods can also have detrimental effects. With certain processed foods, they are manipulated in certain ways (genetic manipulation). It is difficult to understand because they are manipulated to make certain foods more appealing than their original state. As a result, those embellishing characteristics to sell the product make the product not as healthy in the long term.

Yes. There is a great concern here about genetically modified food and particularly seeds.

Yes. We have noted this. We understand genetic manipulation. Your species has learned this, too, at a very preliminary level. In addressing the needs of your planet, often you will manipulate seeds and other organic sources to increase yields to magnify their use as food sources. Sometimes this may have certain unknown negative effects in your early manipulation of genetic materials.

Doc: How much does stress play in the starting of diseases or mental problems and early death?

Stress, in the short term, for brief periods, even moderate stress, is beneficial in extending life. This is part of a survival instinct. However, when there is no external stimulus, and lingering stress persists, it is no longer a survival instinct, but a debilitating, long-term condition, which can affect the longevity of humans. There is a human propensity for stress to linger, grow, and magnify. At that point, this lingering stress creates a vibration or resonance in the human body that has a negative effect. Lingering stress creates a real physical condition for the human body's natural immunity systems to cope with disease. When this is out of balance, the diseases will begin to gain advantage over the human bodies' immune systems. The reduction of stress will create an environment where the natural immunity systems of humans will restore its ability to hold back diseases.

I think that when human beings incur too much stress or prolonged stress, they feel their bodies not being as responsive as they should or they may easily come down with colds and influenzas.

The human mind becomes aware of itself not being as responsive, which, in turn, increases further stress, compounding the issue. The mind is an organ of the body and is connected to the other organs. Each is necessary for a healthy long life. The mind, how it perceives itself and its environment, is very important. It is necessary to have a positive outlook. Optimism is a term you use. This is not just a state of mind, but it is also part of the instinctual normal desire to survive.

Does your species have faculties or aspects that would, if they were introduced into the genetics of man, eventually change the outcome of human progression? What might they be?

Organically?

Yes. Organically.

I feel that our natural telepathic abilities would greatly change the human species in its social behavior. It would produce a great change. It would change many of the institutions, social structures, and methods in which the humans conduct themselves on this planet. There would be certain losses of individuality, but at the same time, there would be a number of positive things. Certain institutions might diminish or go away. It would entail a new understanding about humans themselves and the way they look at each other. Whether their morals or values would change as a result is difficult to predict. When telepathy becomes possible in humans, it is hoped that a new personal threshold of understanding will emerge. The need for police and prisons would diminish or disappear. Communication would be on a level that would create interdependence and understanding to make these institutions less needed.

It would enable early detection of problems, too.

Yes. It would create communication that would touch everyone on a deeply personal level. Concepts of privacy would be radically altered. Initially, each human would experience a fear of loss of individuality. This would be only an illusion in a physical sense. All of what makes humans who you are would remain the same. In a way, your minds would be more interconnected. Humans would feel more naked and exposed. It is hard for us to explain because we are accustomed to this. Our values and our relationships within our species may seem different to humans. Many of the Serpo guests were astonished by this and grew accustomed to it. It would take time for humans, but eventually, they would also become accustomed. That would be one major change.

Don't we already possess the ability of telepathy, but few people use it?

It would be like an organic version of your Internet. On the Internet, there is a trick that humans play on themselves. They think that their thoughts and words are private when they are actually exposed for their whole planet to see. This illusion can sometimes surprise and confound.

It certainly has surprised a few people.

Imagine a telepathic equivalent. Many thoughts, appropriate and inappropriate, would be expressed, to a pervasive degree, among the population. When this happens, a new form of thought discipline would need to be instilled. Humans would take much time to learn this. I feel they would initially have difficulty interacting with each other.

I am sure they would. I remember reading a statement that said, 'Think as though your thoughts are being written across the skies.' That sounded like a good suggestion to me.

Those are wise thoughts. In our society, our social mores and structure are predicated upon that very notion. It is a very wise attitude. If it were possible for telepathy to be available for everyone on your planet, this would need to be understood and embraced. This would be a new way of communicating, but also a new way of interacting with each other that, ultimately, would be very positive in eliminating many of this planet's problems, war, hunger, and politics. Politics would suffer, fortunately. We feel that certain old forms of communication would no longer be necessary. In the short term, it would be very awkward until humans learn new mental disciplines. Ultimately, there would be a higher level of thought and consideration, which would benefit the entire species.

This is an example of how telepathy has made our society as we are. This is also true for many other species on other planets. There is, at present, mostly a lack of telepathy on Earth. Someday, more humans will develop this ability through evolution. Telepathy is very common in the Universe. In this respect, Earth and humans are an anomaly. It is simply where they are at the present rate of their evolution. Part of our fascination with humans is where they are in evolution. Studying humans enables us to learn about ourselves and what we once were. We learned this by observing humans and noticing many situations on Earth that all go back to that one root cause.

There are a few other organic physical aspects of us, that if they were introduced, would create much change on Earth society, but telepathy would be the primary one. Our means of reproduction would probably not be appealing to humans. We have observed human sexuality and that it means many things to humans. Our means of reproduction is more, by human standards, a form of artificial manufacturing. It would also be strange to human society and culture.

It would be, but only, I think, because we are not very telepathic. The sexual aspect also permits closeness between persons. For your culture, 'closeness' is already in place by virtue of your being telepathic.

In many ways, the human intimacy between two human beings, in a deeply personal way, is a foretaste of the telepathy that we commonly enjoy. Our telepathic intimacy extends far beyond just the reasons that humans have for intimacy: love, closeness, or closeness for reproduction. This is just our natural state, our way of being. In a way, we have intimacy at all times, outside of reproduction instincts. Human sexuality is necessary for reproduction, but that is just one small aspect. For the human emotional condition, human sexuality is very important, and in some ways, very predominant in making humanity who you are.

In the origin of our species, we, too, once reproduced in a natural way. We changed to a different means of reproduction, socially controlled, where when one being dies, only then is a new being made to replace that being in our population. As a result, our particular 'psychology' and as you might say, our ancient animal instincts, are still within us, but they have been subdued to a degree to allow more rational and logical thought. To some species, we might seem 'cold,' but we are who we are. We feel this is part of what makes us who we are. It is no worse or better. It is simply different for us and is appropriate for us now. We understand the many aspects of human sexuality and its effects on individuals, as well as society.

From Doc: I would like to give you four key points. This is some-one's version of the conditions that would be required to cause disease. When I have finished listing the four points, I would appreciate your telling us if these are more or less accurate and whether some aspects were missed. He believes the following four conditions must exist to cause disease:

1. hereditary predisposition
2. chronic irritation

3. inciting cause (i.e., a viral infection)
4. catalyst, stress, which makes the whole process begin.

Han: These four conditions, we can understand. It would be, to various degrees, common with all life on Earth, in whatever forms, and on other planets, too. The catalyst, stress, in a way, can be the accumulation of the first three. The catalyst (the fourth condition) can also ultimately be the root cause of the first three. One can manifest the other. However, they are not separate. They are all combined in the process. The second condition is of less concern. The first and third are more predominant in causing the fourth condition. The fourth condition, in turn, causes the first three conditions. I hope I expressed this in a way that is clearly understood.

I do. It is a system, linked together.

It is an interaction and a system. This is correct. You are accurate.

Zeta Reticuli History

I have a question about your home planet. I assume that you live on some other planet, other than your originating planet. I do not know what you consider to be your home. Is it your originating planet or the last planet where you dwelled?

It has a double meaning. Home is where we make it. Yet, at the same time, I understand its other meaning, that it is the point of origin. We all have a point of origin and our home is both. In our minds, it is something we keep and hold dear, wherever we travel. Also, there is a meaning, affection for our point of origin.

Not quite at the beginning of your species, but maybe 20,000 years into your species, in the beginning, what was your society like? This is, of course, before you learned space flight.

These are the humbling thoughts that give our moral framework, balanced against having too much pride, feeling superior over other species, because we know that our humble beginnings are no different from yours. With that in mind, it is how we respectfully interact with other species, knowing that we have had similar childhoods. During our immature period, we behaved similarly as humans do. This was before our telepathic abilities evolved. We can empathize with the human situation for miscommunication and misunderstanding. Our early past was primitive and struggles existed which we eventually overcame. It is an embarrassing part of our life that we thank you for reminding us about. As far as we may seem to have progressed, we still remember our origins.

Was it hunter/gatherer and tribal like?

Yes. This was due, in part, because of our bird-like nature. We congregated in flocks. This was due to competition to survive. We formed into groups of hunter-gatherers and then developed societies and then technology. We eventually formed sophisticated cultural and social behaviors, though they were primitive by current standards.

At what point did your species start building structures? I am talking in terms of years from the beginning of our species.

A million or more in your years.

Assuming that your planet had seas, did your species build primarily along the coasts?

Our planet has always had seas, I am happy to say. It is a critical part of our planet's environment. This makes it similar to your Earth. It is not surprising that the sea, in both situations, made everything else possible, as we understand it.

Was the tendency to build along the waterfronts or to build inland, perhaps in high places? I know that birds like high places.

Birds like high places. Also, their ability to migrate by flight made travel easier to places less accessible to some land creatures. Due to this, being close to the land or the seas was of no consequence. In our own ancient past we migrated freely across oceans and land.

No point of land on your planet was ever too remote?

That is correct.

When your species began building and creating societies, did you go through times of electing people for social order or was that even necessary?

There was a social, to use a human term, 'pecking' order. We understand this, even though we are not, except by our evolutionary heritage, bird-like anymore. We have leaders in our telepathic community. This principle originated in our ancient times and has long been a norm. Our leaders are more accessible than your leaders. The thoughts and projects of our leaders are commonly known through our community through our telepathic connection. We know what our leaders wish and our leaders understand the society they serve. There is much understanding. Your present human biological nature has yet to achieve this. This is all part of the network within the community of mind upon which I have often commented. Many of our early structures were on the surface of the planet. This was an era of transition in which our population grew and reached a point where our environment was becoming threatened.

Perhaps your lives were much shorter then?

Our lives were much shorter. We reached a crisis point where we needed to make great fundamental changes. This was facilitated in part by the evolution of our newfound telepathic abilities. In this era of our planet we changed fundamentally in many ways. One change was relinquishing our normal sexual reproduction as a means of population control. Our species, at that time, had achieved space travel. However, we were still not advanced enough to move whole populations. This change in our means of reproduction was revolutionary. It was not completely accepted at first, as it is now. Only through our emerging telepathy was this great change managed. Telepathy made us see the species for the first time as a whole, not within the context of the individual. Telepathy made us share equally in the burden of these sacrifices for the good of the whole planet, if our species was to survive. It was a very difficult period in our ancient history.

In our society now, when one life passes beyond, only then is another one created. This controls population. Our surface structures retreated from the surface to provide an enjoyable and natural setting on the surface. Our cities moved underground, still connected with the surface, but just underneath. It is a crisis your species, on a planetary scale, has yet to face. If you continue at your present rate, you may not have long to wait. The solution on our planet was successful, in time, and it avoided a planetary catastrophe where natural forces would have reduced population through disease and starvation, putting at risk even the planet itself.

This left the surface to return to its more natural state. Is that what I am hearing?

Yes, one result of this period of great change was the collective realization that we needed to terraform our home planet. We learned, as with our other changes, it took a great sense of unity of purpose to accomplish this. We removed virtually all of our planet's artificial surface structures. We rejected the old ways and returned the surface of the planet back to its original state as we had imagined it in the beginning. Yet, there are great populations under the surface where each has easy access to the surface. They can enjoy the parks and the natural settings on the roofs of our cities.

That is a really interesting idea, and I can see that it is quite viable.

There is less stress now on our planet due to the natural restoration of the surface. There are more plants and forests to sustain our atmosphere now. Our plants and forests no longer have to compete with our population. Food is manufactured on the surface and under the surface as well. As a result, we live in harmony with our home world. Our planet raised our species, now we return that gift back. It also provides an example to our neighbors across space, of what our species values.

May I suggest that you try, if you have not already tried it, something called an Asian pear?

We are fond of apples, as I have mentioned. Asian pears are unique and special in nature. It is a delicacy, like oranges in the Japanese culture, among your Earth cultures. The orange is considered a patriotic symbol to the Japanese. As a dessert with their meals, it is often seen in their diet. We consider Asian pears very special. We often give them as gifts, expressing special regard for another. We have transplanted these trees to other planets. Your Asian pears are often shared at special occasions.

Then I am quite happy you have discovered them. We certainly enjoy them here, too.

It surprises you that we enjoy fruits, like you. Asian pears, particularly, have a unique flavor and texture.

Yes. The texture is like nothing else I have known.

Texture is one quality. It is also appealing and compatible with our ability to masticate this food. It is very comfortable.

Spirituality

No questions in this session.

Contact

Yesterday, I watched a video. This video was about an individual named J-Rod who came from our future. Apparently, he was kept in one of our facilities and was ultimately taken to Los Alamos. Is any of this true?

Yes. This is true. He is a personality that has been selected, tailored for his assignment to be with humans. He is a gateway. He often represents some aspects of this reckless species about which I have warned you. J-Rod is a benevolent being. Do not misunderstand. He has his own agendas and purposes here. Most are not of concern to humans, but can be of concern to our species.

He can move freely through the doorway I mentioned earlier. When in this dimension, he is confined in a biologically-controlled atmosphere and environment. When he leaves and he is on his own planet, it is like stepping from one room in your dwellings on Earth to another room. It is just this easy for him.

Is J-Rod an extraterrestrial or a future human?

J-Rod is, in a sense, an ambassador, and a guide. Also, he is an explorer, exploring your species, as we are. He is not a competitor, but he often has different motives.

Is he also a future human?

J-Rod is both. He is an alien and an extraterrestrial. J-Rod is from another place, but he is also from another time. Part of this is due to the methods of transport and time dilation so, by definition, it does make him from the future. He can see beyond what humans can. He has a relationship with several human scientists, which we feel is positive, and often many of these scientists have grown a sense of affection and affinity for him, too. Humans are beginning to learn certain telepathic abilities through J-Rod, just from their normal interaction.

Frequently, they find themselves surprised that it is really easier than they had foreseen to have these telepathic abilities.

In some crop circles, ferrous materials have appeared inside, but not outside the circles. Can you comment on that?

There is a magnetic residue in the characteristics of authentic crop circles, not the human made ones. This is one feature that some astute humans have discovered in discerning between the human mimics and the authentic crop circles created by off-world species. There is often, in the center of these circles, a focal point where this field is most noticeable. Some humans have even stood in the center of these and interpreted them in either a physical or a spiritual way. They have noticed these energy fields and have tried to be one with them. This is a natural process in knowing that there are means of touching our species beyond the normal physical sense, in a physical way that is not obvious. It is often interpreted as a spiritual experience. It is like, in your physical sense, when one of your aircraft leaves behind a whirlwind that you cannot see, but you can feel and experience it in a very gentle way. I use that analogy to explain what these people often experience in crop circles, a lingering whirlwind or wake. This is like a magnetic wind. These are wakes from these objects, which pass through other dimensions and exist temporarily in these spaces to form these circles on the ground.

I think the word 'wake' is descriptive.

'Wake' is the word for which I was searching. Forgive my inefficiency. Sometimes, in searching for the words, which come through in thought, I have to slow down and express in word terms what often we just share through thought. Forgive my awkwardness. I am, in a way, still learning language in the sense of expressing precisely the proper meaning.

I would not give it a second thought. When we humans speak English, we often flounder and have to search for words.

In a way, we are learning and encompassing all your languages. It is not difficult. It is just difficult in making sure the right term is used in the proper situation.

In the sentence structures that you use, sometimes the subject and verb are reversed, as they are in German, but having studied German, I catch the flow.

This is correct. Good for you. It is in language, trying to address considerately, the right language in the right situation with the right person so that they understand and we understand.

Yes. I imagine that working through language is a slow process.

It is not difficult. As is in the human case, theory and practice are two different things. (Smiles.)

Do you know the name Bob Lazar?

Yes.

In what context?

He was connected to S-4, a place with a doorway at a facility that contained a workshop for interaction between your species and others, including ours. We are aware of this.

In that space, we understand that there is equipment. One is called a 'quantum viewing device cube' that is used to look into probable futures. Is that a true?

Say again.

Quantum viewing cube, to look into probable futures.

Yes. We are aware of this. This is a subject that makes us very concerned. If controlled by the species that placed it there to share with humans, we are not concerned. It can foretell certain possible parallel futures. It is a doorway to an infinite variety of dimensions. In time, in creating alternate paths of beginnings and outcomes, it can create certain paradoxes, if not handled responsibility.

Well, that concerns me right away.

Its appearance to humans is one of a small and innocuous device. However, it has great power. It should be regarded with great care. It should not be one to be feared, but it is one that needs to be much more understood so that its use does not permanently alter what humans regard as their reality.

My concern is not for the device, but for human beings who use it.

That is our concern, too. I feel that this is an artifact, a legacy of an alien culture that may have acted inappropriately by sharing too much too soon.

Are they still interacting with us?

Yes. This species is the same species that is irresponsibly abducting humans. This species acts recklessly, but in human terms, their gifts, in exchange for human abductions, may be perceived as positive. This cube is to be respected. You have a term, 'playing with fire.' However, it could also be a device of great promise. My comments are to inform, not place a value.

Is there also a device there called a Gimbal device, a kind of looking glass, as we call it? It might also be used as a star gate.

Yes. This is often regarded as a simulator for our craft. Our craft are not just objects that fly through your atmosphere or in space. They can fly through dimensions. It is part of what we use to fold gravity and other forces. It is like a ground test vehicle for simulating how our craft operate. It works not just in this physical dimension, but it is also a doorway through other dimensions. This is how our craft move from one place to another, across great distances. This device, when oriented at an attitude, will also facilitate a doorway for transport of certain beings. We have different species, including our own, transporting to S-4, and departing from S-4. It is my earlier reference to S-4 also being a doorway. It is through these devices that this is facilitated.

How did we humans acquire that Gimbal device?

Through the reckless species, the others, along with the cube device.

If one opens this device, will this open a second timeline?

Yes. It could open many different timelines. This is the danger that we would want to warn about. It could also be a great gift in avoiding certain existing timelines. Some timelines can be replayed with a different outcome, one that can be positive for humans as they understand the positive or negative in their own situation. It is a different alternative line. It is part of the quantum mechanics of time and dimensions. They are of great importance in that they are what we use in our normal existence. It would be like giving a primitive culture advanced technology for which they are perhaps not yet ready.

The species that introduced this was reckless in demonstrating this technology to humans at this present time. Humans, once aware of it (this technology) greatly desired it, once they understood its abilities. In bargaining between humans and this reckless species, this resulted in exchanging this technology for many human abductions. They feel that genetic material is so important to them that they would exchange such technology of such great power with humans. Still, admittedly, it is under the control of these reckless aliens. This reckless species uses these devices as portals, and can easily renege on their agreement, taking away their technology along with their acquired human genetic materials at any time. This has not happened. We have often debated within our own species whether this was appropriate or equitable exchange of technology for access to genetic material.

That would be a good argument.

It is a controversial issue upon which you have touched. We have privately not made humans too aware of the discussions among ourselves regarding this reckless species, as I will politely refer to them.

Since a timeline could be rerun, if something catastrophic occurred as a result of this technological exchange, could it perhaps be undone? Is that what I am hearing?

I am reluctant to say this. Admittedly, yes, this is true. It is not a panacea. When there is a change in a timeline, it affects many timelines, but only to a certain radius out from the change or anomaly across time. It has certain naturally limiting, but also quantum effects, too. The true extent of the introduction of any new timeline may not be as apparently different as humans might perceive. Certain detailed and key elements might be altered in a way that would definitely change, in a local sense, certain local timelines.

The Universe

No questions in this session.

Other

I ask now about the properties of gold. Does gold have a reflective aspect that we do not know about right now? Apparently, it was used in a kind of web inside of a suit, for what purpose I am not certain. Could you help us understand this concept about gold's reflective nature, and how it might be used within that context?

Gold has many properties for conducting electrical energy or in thermodynamic properties in absorbing heat, and releasing heat. It has certain characteristics, which separates itself from other minerals. At the atomic level, gold is unique unto itself. In addition, it has a way of conducting energies, beyond electrical, that humans will soon discover. In an interactive way, it acts in both changing and shaping energy around it. These can be useful in future technologies that will benefit humans. Earth has much gold yet to be taken from the planet for use.

Many times, other alien species have come to Earth to discretely mine the mineral to use for their own purposes. This particular solar system has a higher than usual proportion of gold, along with many other elements such as aluminum and iron. These are useful in many ways, some of which humans have yet to discover. The amount of gold humans use on Earth accumulates. Humans do give great value to gold's lasting properties. All the gold that has ever been mined by humans, whether in the past or in the present, even from ancient times, still exists today, in some form. Humans find the properties of gold to be of value. Other planetary cultures easily make use of gold. It is easily accessible for use in many things, technology for example.

As you know, we, and other cultures, use gold for jewelry. We do not currently know about the extra properties of gold that you mentioned. Does wearing gold jewelry have any effect on the human body because of these extra properties?

No. In relation to humans, it is fairly inert. It has properties that make it useful for many functions, both for vanity and for purposes of replacing certain parts of human bodies, such as dental applications.

Open Session for Comments or Questions

Do you have any further comments before I begin to close this session?

I wish to reach out to touch you in a gentle way. Do I have your permission?

Yes. (This was a nervous 'yes,' the therapist being uncertain of what was to come.)

It is only a form of communication that I wish to place in you. It is a message for all of my species and other species that you may encounter. Presently, and wherever your spirit and energy travel, both physically and beyond, know that you have a home and are always welcome on our worlds. Know that others will see you as a being that is one with us. You are one who understands the communication we share. We hope that more like you will eventually participate. This is a letter of introduction for others to recognize you and to give you great respect and hospitality wherever you may choose to go in your personal travels across time and space, wherever your soul should go. In that, I now conclude my time here today.

Thank you for that gift. I accept it with gratitude. (Therapist is astonished at being given such a gift! There was only the sensation of a faint fluttering in the skull membrane.)

Until we meet again.

Session XIII, Anunnaki, Cell Talk, Brain Comparisons
October 22, 2011

Steve was inducted and given some therapy. The therapist invited the being known as Han to step forward. It took a little longer than usual. The therapist asked Steve to describe what he was seeing.

Therapist asks Steve, 'Has he come to join us?'

Steve: Yes. Han is there.

Are we staying where we are or is he going to set up a new environment for us?

Steve: Initially, we were together on a stage at my old high school, and we were happy to see each other, but the surroundings seemed inappropriate. We have moved to your living room in our minds, and we are now comfortable. We are in a very warm and comfortable setting. Han is petting your Sheltie, stroking its back, and now he is sitting down in a chair. The Sheltie responds happily as she would to any other, enjoying Han's petting. Han looks rather spindly, but he is not unpleasant to look at, just different. Han's form has its own beauty and I am just marveling at the opportunity to experience this. His form is elegant in a very different way. His joints and hands are long and spindly. The joints in his arms are close to humans, but they do not have the same proportions, as they would be in a human. They are very similar, but different. He does not look too skeletal-like, but there is a little suggestion of that. He seems to be very comfortable. Each of us is in a separate chair. He is just being patient, and I think he is reading our thoughts, and he is sending back his appreciation for the welcome. He says he is ready to begin our conversation.

Thank you Steve. Steve, would you kindly step back now completely out of his way so that he may come through clearly and without any residual energy. Han, when you are ready, we most cordially welcome you.

Hello, Mary. This is Han.

Thank you. You are, of course, quite welcome.

Thank you for the invitation again.

As usual, I have many questions.

I am smiling.

(Therapist laughs.)

Earth History

You are familiar with what we call 'cold fusion.' What is the real story of cold fusion? Is this a real discovery?

Cold fusion is a path of only limited possibilities. Cold fusion is a false scientific premise often used as a means for humans to create income for themselves by imagining processes that are not technically feasible. Sometimes these are used as deceptions to create income for individuals and people who believe in such free energy possibilities. Many theories of physics related to cold fusion are not possible in sustaining physical reactions. In the Universe, there is little that is not possible. However, cold fusion, by human perception, should be looked at with some skepticism. Energy is everywhere in the Universe. It exists in many forms, nuclear, chemical, kinetic forms, among others. Energy manifests itself by continually transforming from one form into another. Matter is energy, and energy is matter - times the speed of light squared.

Thank you. I know that we are not able to replicate the original cold fusion experiments so that certainly creates skepticism.

Do you see the human species eventually using the full capacity of their brains, and if so, how might that change us?

You will, eventually, if your ability to survive on your planet continues. Your mind capacity will increase. Your interpretation of what full capacity is may include areas of the human brain you still have yet to discover. One indication of this will be a gradual ability to become telepathic. Mental telepathy is a common trait among many advanced life forms. In the Universe, it is a common way of communicating. Eventually, humans will slowly develop this capacity, and when you do, it will change your connectivity with other species on other planets, and your relationships among yourselves. There will be greater collective insights and understanding. This will create great changes in your society. It will fundamentally change the structure of your world.

Thank you. Are you familiar with the works of an author named Zecharia Sitchin who translated ancient Sumerian texts? The very old Sumerian texts talked about the Anunnaki coming to this planet to find gold. They found primitive human beings whom they changed genetically so that they could use them for workers to mine gold. Is this true?

The Sumerians were an important contributor to the human species early in its history. Their great awareness of the sky and the great precision in which they recorded certain celestial events is quite noteworthy. Part of this is due to the visitations of the Anunnaki and their heightened awareness. The Sumerians came to the realization of the need to record their history in detail. They had an appreciation for many things. The Sumerians were often seen in a rather abstract or in an apprehensive way. However, they created and contributed much to the early ancient understanding about humans and the Universe. Many of the Sumerians, and other cultures, too, had contact with the beings they referred to as the Anunnaki. The Anunnaki desired certain materials from your planet, such as gold, for use in their technology.

Was the Sumerian language already in place at the time of contact or was it learned from an outside culture?

It was spoken prior to contact and was modified by an outside culture later. Looking back in your time, across linear time, you see both influences. In the beginning, the Sumerians created a precise and sophisticated language. It was much like Greek is today, with very specific meanings for words. The Anunnaki widened the Sumerian vocabulary later, when the Anunnaki introduced themselves to them.

Was this a cooperative meeting or did the humans ultimately wind up serving the Anunnaki?

The Anunnaki initially imposed themselves in very remote places. Gradually, the Anunnaki became more prevalent in the Sumerian society. In turn, the Sumerians had to submit and accept the advanced nature of the Anunnaki. It soon became apparent that it would be beneficial for both. One advanced civilization displaced the less advanced civilization. When the Anunnaki realized that their need for certain raw materials was satisfied, they erased much of their own presence in Sumerian society, and as a result, the Sumerian culture collapsed into your history.

Was there any genetic material introduced into the human species at that time?

Yes. Some Anunnaki were able to leave their mark in the Sumerian heritage and this modified the human structure, some of which is buried (in genetic code). It will only become apparent in man's future when they become more telepathic. The contribution of the Anunnaki from long in the past will then manifest itself in a positive, unexpected way.

Some people have very strong immune systems and other people seem to have vulnerable immune systems. Other than heredity, what factors might contribute to these differences?

Primarily it is heredity, but it is also environmental factors. Exposures to certain environments help to bolster the immune system by creating stronger abilities to resist infection and disease.

Are we able to talk specifically to our own cells and send them the message to be resilient and strong?

Our science has the ability to heal more effectively in that we can program individual cells to focus on specific tasks beyond their own already existing autonomic roles. We use this to help in resisting certain diseases, such as cancer, that we talked about earlier. For other heredity diseases, humans would benefit greatly by this. At present, due to our limited contact with humans, we do not have the opportunity to administer such medicine or abilities extensively within your population. The concept is not a unique one, but we can put it into practice very effectively. Perhaps humans will someday learn this ability, too.

To your knowledge, does our military or any other world military or governmental agency use implants in human beings without their knowledge for purposes of tracking or any other purposes?

We have noticed in certain intelligence agencies, for their own safety, they will incorporate implants within their agents so that their position is known for their own protection. We have also noticed this in other countries with similar intelligence functions. We are well aware of the secrets of many intelligence organizations due to our telepathic ability. We can read the minds of many and we harbor most secrets that many agencies hold dear for their own sense of security. Many share the same secrets, each unaware the other possesses the same secrets. Ultimately, military secrets are often the least secret. Human origin implants are used on a limited basis. These are primitive compared to ours. Ours work in an organic fashion. They have a benign appearance. As such, they disguise themselves. Our implants enhance natural brainwave patterns which humans are unable to register. The human mind sends out energy and we can detect these naturally occurring waves of energy.

Many species will use these energy waves to track abductees. They work as a form of radio transmitter to radiate a location. Human implants are not a transceiver. They do not receive, only transmit. Alien forms of implants invariably can monitor human subjects in ways you might consider very invasive. Metabolic body functions, the subject's thoughts, retrieved memories, and even new memories can be implanted and monitored. Some species can observe the human condition in ways your expectation of individuality might find uncomfortable. In contrast, human agency implants are more rare, and are mainly so their own people can be located if they are in a compromising situation and require assistance for their safety.

Are you familiar with a species of wolf acting in a bipedal manner? There have been a hundred or more sightings of wolves seen walking in a bipedal manner. Witnesses say they are in Wisconsin and Michigan. It is not that they look particularly different from a wolf, but their bipedal behavior is quite surprising.

This may be. We have noticed this on rare occasions. They stand on their hind legs. This is an anomaly.

Do you think it might be an evolutionary testing behavior?

It is yet to be determined. Their ability to pursue game or to flee from danger is still more effective on their four legs instead of their two hind legs, but it is an interesting development. When the forelegs begin to use tools, this will then be interesting, unexpected development. The combination of the more prevalent hind legs and a different use for the forelegs would indicate more conclusively that a new genetic or evolutionary path may have begun. Time will tell. Humans and we will continue to observe what develops.

George and I have a strong interest in ancient history on this planet and the development of various cultures. Could you give us a little overview and perhaps bring out points that we would not have suspected.

About human history?

Yes.

One important element that is not yet fully appreciated, but is growing rapidly, is the effect of many influences from space on human history. Many more asteroid impacts have occurred that have radically changed the cultures and environments of your planet than you first thought. In particular, many areas of your world, which were lush with growth, but are now deserts, due to impacts with asteroids and comet-like objects. These have had a profound impact on how the world is seen today. There were times, before these impacts, when it was quite different. The Sahara area of your planet is largely desert. Before that, it was a garden. Other areas of the Middle East were in a similar condition. This was very recent, as little as five or six thousand Earth years ago, that these events occurred. There might be certain events you have not yet considered in how you view your ancient times from your perspective today.

Zeta Reticuli History

You mentioned once that sometimes, when you have a social gathering, you exchange a gift of fruit or something else.

A number of things.

What kind of events do you have that would bring your people together in a physical gathering? What kind of celebrations or events do you have?

Sometimes, when a new life is brought into existence, we celebrate. Usually, when the old one passes on to another existence that you call dying, we gather. There may be the celebration of new discoveries or new relationships within our species, individually as well as collectively. Sometimes gifts are for other species. We often mark periods of time in our history and in our own personal lives. It is not a personal life in the way perhaps that you understand personal, but personal, magnified by the community around us. We often will use these special times for such gifts and times of connecting together with friends.

If this is not too personal, do you have the same organs as the human species? If so, do you have any additional ones or have some of them changed in their functions?

You may notice that often we do not wear certain garments. We often wear garments to enhance our telepathic abilities. For example, we may wear them in our exploratory missions to enhance our awareness of the environment that we are exploring. We wear clothing for exploration, but also for protection. These are designed so they do not inhibit part of our respiration. We have lungs, as you call them. They do not fulfill their role completely. We are also able to respirate through our skin and exude waste products. This is a supplemental part of our lung capacity within our physiology. Therefore, we often do not wear garments because these may inhibit our ability to respirate efficiently. Also, our gender organs are not apparent in our physical appearance. This is partially due to a merging of genders, but both characteristics exist.

In our species, one gender is less apparent and this is partially due to our means of current reproduction being an artificial one. Our gender organs become less important. They are a legacy from an earlier time. I have commented on our bone structure. It is both light and strong with a 'Kevlar-like' weave, as you call it, for added strength. This originated from a bird-like missing link in our long evolutionary past. Our minds have increased in capacity, in both size and usage. With this came the telepathic abilities that we have grown to depend upon.

Do you have frontal lobes and a kind of similar structure to the human brain?

Yes. We have areas of our mind that serve different functions. We have frontal lobes and a cerebral cortex with a similar nature and purpose as humans.

The area of the brain that would be highly developed would be the portion that enables spoken language. Has that diminished in your brain because of your ability to be telepathic? Perhaps it has increased?

It has diminished, but due to our telepathic ability, our memory capacity has increased to store in memory the greater volume of communication. The language centers of our brains have been displaced, to a degree by this. On many different levels, we are able to project energy in a quantum way between our minds, both in short distances and through special training, across great distances to other stars, similar to what is happening here with us.

Because of your ability to send energy, do you also use it as a mechanism for healing?

Yes. We have learned this and we have specialized entities within our species for this purpose. I mentioned earlier about beings that could be considered doctors or scientists with certain abilities, one of which you could call medicine. These beings can focus these energies, as well as use physical instrumentalities to heal. The two are used in concert. We can interrupt pain signals to the brain. These energies can be transmitted to other beings to help heal as well.

Concerning your glands, your heart, and your liver, would you care to talk to us about them?

We have to metabolize the food we eat. We still eat food and there are waste products. We often have to store these nutrients in various forms that the body makes for itself. In the basic elements there are fats and sugars that we metabolize. These are more plant fats, not animal fats. We are not carnivores. We mainly have vegetables and fruits as our food sources. We respect those who need, perhaps, other sources for their diet. Our sources are sufficient for us. Our bodies are able to metabolize these. We have certain digestive organs. Our reproductive organs become less important due to our other form of artificial reproduction. Many species who also follow this form of reproduction will sometimes abduct humans to supplement their genetic stock from species genetically similar to them that follow the more natural forms of reproduction.

Can't they just use the genetic material without using the human surrogate?

For purposes of hybridization, a surrogate is often required. For genetic material alone, often a surrogate is not needed. At times, certain ova and sperm are taken and genetically altered to suit the needs of the species who need to maintain their ability to be a viable species in their continuing existence.

What about your heart? How does that compare to the human heart?

We have heart organs. Our heart has a different number of chambers. We do have a circulatory and lymphatic system similar to humans. These organs are in a different, but similar location in the chest area. We have a sternum and a kind of rib bone framework that protects the heart and lung areas, much like humans do. Our hearts have reduced and changed in their capacity from our early evolution when we were more bird-like, and we needed to respirate more. Our heart rate no longer requires as high a rate of respiration as it did in the past. Our bodies, in comparison to humans, may seem more frail. Our current hearts are well suited to our present state of evolution.

You are familiar with human beings when they take someone's pulse. Can you tell us what your heart rate is per minute?

Our heart rate at rest is 90 to 120 beats per minute. It is rapid compared to humans.

I am surprised. I would have thought, with your longevity, your pulse rate would run slower.

This is due to our heart capacity being smaller than your heart capacity. It is of a design that has a number of redundancies. These redundancies contribute to our relative longevity. Where one chamber may become deficient, another will compensate. Two hearts in one may be one way to understand it. This design was genetically engineered and incorporated in our distant past.

Has your liver become smaller over time because your skin is respirating some of your waste?

Yes. The form of liver that we have stores sugars that are available to us in case our bodies require it. Our 'liver-like' organ, as you refer to it, is for both metabolizing and storage. It gives us added energy at certain times. It is not too dissimilar than humans. Humans also store sugars in their liver, as we understand human physiology, but perhaps not to the same extent.

Spirituality

Why did the Catholic Church invent the concept of saints?

In your religious history, there are many bureaucracies around your planet in various cultures. Frequently, there is a human need to control how God is seen. Concerning the concept of God and how it applies to the individual, often churches will act as intermediaries. Saints are sometimes created as part of this structure. This was to create a formality and structure in many religions. Saints are often created to honor the past works of those who have served God. This is how their works have been interpreted through history. Particularly in the Catholic Church, there were many ancient texts, religious books, Luke, Mark, John and others. Four main ones were decided upon in the early Christian Church. This was done to politically and spiritually unify the early Church. As a result, other books that were as important, some of which have been recently discovered in Earth archaeology, have been excluded. This was due to the early decision made regarding how the Catholic Church and others would structure their theology. Perhaps, in a less mystical way, this may have also created this church as an impersonal intermediary when other views were to have a personal relationship with God. We have observed this in your culture.

It has always been my impression that we can talk to anyone we wish to on the spiritual side and I am puzzled by this need for an intermediary.

It is for the intermediary's agenda, not God's agenda. We, too, believe in a higher spiritual being. Though you perceive our culture and perhaps see us as highly advanced, we are still, in many ways, asking the same fundamental questions. As we gaze out upon the Universe and the stars, we see how the workings of the Universe came about. It only makes us wonder how this was created, as we observe the amazing ability of physics in the Universe. Part of our nature is to look coldly and objectively in a scientific manner. Still, there is a part of us that retains an ancient instinct to wonder what is beyond what we do not understand. We also find emotion infused into our concepts of what reality is for us. It often makes us wonder about a creator of the Universe, as well. We can empathize with the human need for this in whatever form humans wish to express their spirituality.

There is a spiritual concept that when human adventurers or explorers reach out for more knowledge, a spiritual entourage attaches to them so that they, too, may learn. Are you familiar with this concept?

The spirit's desire to explore is a desire to celebrate life. This celebration is to learn all that one can learn and to explore the unknown. We, as spacefarers, embrace this concept. We would spiritually die if we did not have this desire to reach out to the stars. In reaching out to the stars, we reach out to other life, too. There are wonders to discover and learn about. In concert with this, to surround oneself with similar elements, in a spiritual way, would make much sense. For the bold, they take with them a spiritual protection against the unknown. This is a mysterious protection, not closed, but spiritually open to new ideas and concepts. The desire to explore and be in spiritual harmony makes sense.

What could you tell us about the afterlife of your species? Is it something that is co-created?

Co-created?

Yes. That would be where your thought forms and thought forms from another source unite, creating a type of environment for an afterlife, if that, in fact, occurs.

We believe in an afterlife, in a spiritual context and in a physical sense. We have an understanding that there is an infinite variety of dimensions in the physical Universe. This is both a scientific fact and a belief. In many beliefs, these become facts. We know that in the community of mind among our species the interconnectiveness becomes more apparent when one passes on. Their identity leaves behind a lingering wake. Often, the loss is greater for those left behind than for the being that has passed on. This is true for you, too, is it not? They go to a higher place, a different place. With our telepathic abilities and the interconnectiveness, this facilitates a greater understanding of what could be beyond. It is part of our belief system that beings transcend and continue in another place, on a different level. Additionally, like all forms of energy in the Universe, it transforms, once again. What you call souls, we believe we have souls, too. We have not discussed souls much, but we have often mentioned it. It is natural to assume that we each share these concepts. Aliens, as you refer to us, have souls, too. The term alien is transitory, too, from the unknown to becoming the familiar. I hope I have expressed it in an understandable way.

I think what I am hearing is that your belief is that the environment in the afterlife already exists. Is that correct?

Yes. We often transcend to another dimension. This is where we cross over to another level of existence.

I suspect, from what you have been telling me, human souls and the souls of other species will be able to interact, especially since you know Dr. Mack's soul.

Yes. 'The Courageous One' is what we call him. He was brave, among his peers, in seeing clearly and understanding early, that what he was seeing was entirely new in the context of the educational institutions of which he was a part. He stood out from the rest. He declared that there was a mystery to be explored and this was a great doorway for exploration if humans take note of the abduction phenomenon. This applied in the context of 'visitors' in general, too, whether their intent is malevolent or benevolent. He drew attention to this. We call him the 'Courageous One.'

It took his unusual credentials, really, to give him the ability to be published, and to be heard.

He was a beautiful human being who could see beyond the problem and could take into account a possibility of other realities, which are commonplace to us. He was a Columbus in your culture, to use a term. Because of his status among his peers, he was a controversial and brave soul, and we were saddened at his untimely loss.

Was his death an accident?

Yes. Dr. Mack was known to us and, he was an 'absent minded professor.' He was deep in thought, often oblivious to the goings on around him of the normal paces of life, such as your dangerous automobile traffic.

That I certainly understand.

It was a tragic accident. It was not premeditated.

I only met him for a few moments. Of course, he was very cordial. What I picked up from him was his being deep in thought, but also having a sense of sadness.

His sadness was partly because he knew he was only embarking at the beginning of something and he knew he had much left to understand. Dr. Mack knew his journey of discovery, if the correct path, was not an easy one. Is this not always the case? In human terms, his life did not afford him the time to understand more. His academic position allowed him great freedom to explore these new avenues. The beauty among his many skills was expressed particularly with compassion for the abductees, as well as for your children, as in the case in Africa where a species visited a school. He was a beneficial contributor in making visitor contact more comfortable for humans. He created reassurance and understanding for these contactees. I hope my thoughts are not fragmented.

I am doing pretty well with the translation.

We talked a little bit about energy, and that the soul, being of energy, could not be destroyed. Does a soul experience something like reincarnations?

The souls often translate to other dimensions. In those other dimensions they may take on a physical form again, perhaps in a different form. This probably could be interpreted as 'reincarnation.' We often refer to it as renewal, but the meaning is the same.

Contact

Not during this session, but a later session, would it be possible to use remote viewing to take us to observe a hybrid culture off planet?

Yes. This is possible. There are hybrids that exist here (Earth) too, though they are limited in number and their period of time is limited. We spoke of this earlier. The hybrid represents a transition in a continuing process to adapt to live naturally in this environment and to blend in to the human population. The more they become adapted, the more human they become. The part of them that is alien soon becomes displaced into the less dominate role. Many of their advanced natural abilities as an alien species are lost. One goal of hybridization is to retain their preexisting natural abilities, while adapting into the existing Earth habitat. The compromise of hybridization often negates its real purpose. To become human, they lose some abilities that aliens enjoy.

Did they volunteer for that?

There is no sense of individualism. It is part of what is expected. In some ways they are selected and have no choice. It is the way of some species. They are made to adapt to act as the vanguard beings or scouts. I would not call it an invasion, merely integration into human society for many mutually beneficial purposes.

The Universe

No questions in this session.

Other

No questions in this session.

Open Session for Comments or Questions

Do you have anything that you would like to comment on or suggest at this time before I bring Steve back?

Your world is going through a number of changes. Of concern is the population growth of your planet. I see many of the same circumstances that once confronted our world with overpopulation. Even though the population of your planet is not evenly distributed, the concentrations of populations overall still create a burdensome effect on the natural abilities of the planet to accommodate such large populations. I fear that a time will come when, through disease or starvation, your population will have to stabilize naturally on its own. You will need to adjust to the new circumstances that such a large population would create. It is important that your planet and all the species that live on the planet are not stressed beyond their existing capacity. You still act individually. If the existing solar cycles on this planet continue, there could be an intersection of many factors, overpopulation, global warming, and the disappearance of many species displaced by human populations. Those displaced species provide many medicines for your own species.

Part of our reason for being in touch with you is to monitor, and, without your knowledge, help your planet continue to be the garden of great diversity, abundance, and life that it is known for by many species. Your planet is a garden that needs to be preserved. In the opinion of many species, the survival of the human species remains in doubt, due to its overpopulation and continued growth. Overpopulation is the danger that we would like to see avoided.

As would we.

I feel that I also wish to leave you with a sense of optimism. Have no fear of the future. Create the ability to make changes.

Thank you for your generosity in giving us knowledge and insights. We look forward to meeting with you again.

I wish to end our session on what could be, not what has to be. In time, the planet will correct itself. If the beneficial understanding is found early, and the corrections and adaptations made before the Earth's natural way takes a more cruel solution, your species will be successful. On that note, I wish to conclude our conversation.

Until we meet again.

I look forward to our next communication at the appropriate time. Thank you for the invitation.

Thank you and good night.

Session XIV, Music, Hibernation, Duality, Sentinels
October 30, 2011

Steve was inducted and given some therapy. Han was invited to step forward. Steve was restless and it took a little longer than usual.

Steve: I see trees.

Therapist: I feel a fluttering in my third eye, which is an indication of telepathy. Han will, because of our limitations, speak orally through Steve, but he is also speaking telepathically to both of us.

Steve: It is harder to find him this time. It is kind of murky.

He is just moving us into a different setting.

Steve: I am trying not to be too anxious. I have to get rid of that. (Long sigh.) I am trying to relax.

Just be an observer. That is all. Focus on the place between your eyebrows. You may feel a kind of fluttering, almost like soft butterfly wings. He has some big things today.

Steve: That's better.

Yes. He says that the best communication is effortless and for you to remain in an effortless state of mind as we continue with our sessions. There will be new experiences, so, to make these more available, remain in an effortless state of mind. I can feel his affection and even his enjoyment in wanting to take us to these new places and experiences.

Han, when you are ready, please let us know.

Yes. I am ready.

Earth History

No questions in this session.

Zeta Reticuli History

I would like to talk to you about the autonomic system. Are you able to slow down your heart rate and respiration, not for sleep, but to go into a state of hibernation?

We often slow down our autonomic reflexes when we are telepathic. In human terms, it might be considered a form of meditation. At present, my abilities (autonomic responses) are slowed down already. This comes unconsciously. It is possible to slow down our autonomic rates. Frequently, young, teenager forms of our species, to use your term, use this ability as a game among themselves, slowing down their vital signs. They use it to frighten the older ones. It is just the young ones being challenging and rebellious. We have more in common than we first revealed. It is often used as a kind of game. However, it is also a game that ultimately has a useful purpose.

Mischievous is what I call it. (Therapist laughs about the thought of alien children playing this game.)

Mischievous is a good word. At times, this can be a good survival trait in situations where, in order to survive until we can be rescued, it can be used as a form of survival technique. It is what children of our species use for mischief, when they slow their autonomic systems down to what might be considered near death. They always come back, but they learn a useful tool to perhaps use later on in life. Sometimes the concern with the young ones is their lack of discipline and experience that naturally occurs at that age. They learn that they do no harm to themselves when they dare to take their autonomic reflexes dangerously low. Many of our species are welcome to follow and explore new thoughts. Often, they will mediate and contemplate deep thoughts about many things in the Universe, science, mathematics and physics.

Do they also contemplate music?

Yes. We do have music in our culture, and it is so in many other planetary cultures. Music is many things to many species. Music has a deep impact on our existence because our very origin is connected with sound. In a way, all objects in the Universe are created in a resonance of vibrations. Many of these vibrations are sound vibrations. Music is, in a way, a universal language.

You anticipated my next question.

If used intelligently, music can nourish and heal. There is a strange and unusual connection between mathematics and music. Music is the only art form where its unique form and the medium are the same.

Yes. We have noted the connection, but I do not know how to describe it. It has a balance and exploration seems to be a part of it.

Mathematics is the only science where the method and the subject are uniquely the same. Mathematics can only be studied by using mathematics.

Indeed.

Music is only created and experienced as music so there is a natural connection between mathematics and music. Both are experienced as pure objects of the brain by your species and by many other species of the Universe. Only through these artificial connections does the method of music and mathematics have meaning that extends beyond one mind to another mind.

It is very interesting how jazz musicians work with each other. In what might seem like chaos on the surface, they automatically, as a group, almost telepathically, synchronize and create a structure.

It is a beneficial exercise both to the music makers and to the listeners to enjoy. It is a celebration of this communication in a way that seems an alternate to normal communications. We are not unfamiliar with this. Some of our musical instruments are different and they create sounds with many unique properties. The music though, in patterns and rhythms, is not dissimilar to human music. I mentioned Mozart earlier, but there are many others, by your contemporary view, who reflect multiple layers of communication. In many ways, it is not dissimilar to telepathic thought where many rhythms of thought and emotions are expressed simultaneously, particularly in forms that you refer to as classical music. The great range of emotions (emoted by classical music) surpasses some other forms of human music, which are just as beautiful in their own right.

Music creates a sympathetic vibration and enhances our emotional vibration.

There is a strange interpretation by intelligent minds that enjoy that resonance. We, too, can enjoy these vibrations. Humorously, humans who do not enjoy mathematics often *count* while they are enjoying music. When humans enjoy music, they are unconsciously enjoying mathematics. Mathematics is a true universal language, but music follows very closely in spiritual harmony. It is not a surprise that the form and function of each are the same.

I would like, at some other time, to have a more detailed conversation with you about mathematics and music.

I will try to answer your questions.

You have been very kind.

Spirituality

No questions in this session.

Contact

Han, Steve told me earlier you were in a forest. Did you take us to this place because of our request last time to visit a hybrid culture?

No. I took us there to help Steve temporarily relax until we could go to that place that I promised we would visit together.

Yes. He is rather excited today.

He is having problems visiting this particular time and he does not know why. He apologizes. He is quite comfortable now so we will go to the other place with him.

Yes. He so enjoys it. There is so much on the agenda I scarcely know where to start.

The hybrid world is available for us to visit. We can also visit hybrids here at this place you call Earth, if you choose.

Wherever there is a culture, we would be happy to visit. Please, let's go ahead with that process, if you would be kind enough to describe that for us. By the way, I did feel the pulsing in my forehead, just to acknowledge. Yes, we would very much enjoy it, so, if you will be so kind, thank you.

We are on Earth, in a college setting, like a fraternity house. The students in this house are all hybrids. They are a little cell unto themselves. In the isolation of this house, they are comfortable among themselves. It is their 'away' place where they can feel solitude while taking steps to venture out into this planet's society. It is their retreat where they live. There are four hybrids living here, one female and three males. They live together, each in their separate rooms. They communicate with each other telepathically and they can communicate with us. They are about college age in appearance. They often wear sunglasses and other disguises because their features, though human, still have a certain strange appearance. Their features are such that other students on the street and in the community might find them striking. They are trying to blend in. They are not lonely. They have each other. This has been arranged this way so they can help assimilate themselves into the culture. They often have a pale complexion that is not too dissimilar from many humans of that age who often wear strange clothes and also display such a complexion. So, they can blend into this setting without much difficulty.

Outside of this community they might be a little more striking. They seem to be accepted. It is a Berkeley community setting with a lot of old rustic homes used as fraternity and sorority houses. They cannot wear tattoos or pierced jewelry. These are abhorrent in hybrid society. It would also quickly reveal their identity by having such local tribal cultural ornaments applied. I am not sure they are connected with the University. It is just a house in which they live. They seem to be getting nutrients and food from outside sources brought by frequent alien visitors. They also seem to be eating some human foods, fruit in particular, and other things that help them cross over. They are rather thin and they wear normal clothing – jeans, shirts, and blouses. They often wear sunglasses outside, not for protection, but to conceal their eyes that look a bit striking to humans. They are rather dark and slanted. The images of 'aliens' on book covers and other sources has permeated human culture to such an extent that they could be easily recognized. Perhaps they might be recognized as hybrids. They wear sunglasses to help conceal this.

Did they arrive at their destination as young adults?

They were created aboard a craft through genetic engineering. Then, as children, they were placed in a home where they could transition be exposed to other humans. They looked similar to humans so the main sense is to learn the ways and actions of humans. Their behavior patterns, like language slang, and motivations seem awkward. It has often been commented that hybrids seem awkward in your society. In recent times, this has been the primary focus to help this awkwardness disappear.

This added level of integration requires more time to blend in perfectly. It is a reflection of the hybrid program that integration is sufficiently successful when humans never seem to be aware of such a being in their midst. Yet, we still recognize each other.

With the hybrids that are there, I can communicate with them telepathically. They seem to be aware of us now and are not concerned because I am here as an intermediary, as a guest to telepathically assure them that their identities have not been exposed. They maintain a certain privacy and secrecy only for the alarm that it might cause to some humans surrounding them in the community. They seem to be working in some jobs. Some are attending school. The ones in school are doing very well. They learn very quickly. Their instructors regarded them as very gifted.

Is it not a concern that they might appear as too gifted?

I understand. They are conscious of this and try not to be scholastically perfectly. The knowledge is already known, but it is important to learn it in a human context, which can be slow, and in some ways they are impatient with this. They compensate by learning the social skills within the classroom and with the instructor. They avoid the cafeterias mainly because the food is not much to their liking and they are very selective. The social situations are less controlled in the cafeterias where they could appear less adaptable to unexpected events around them. The classroom is a setting, by contrast, that is somewhat controlled where the focus is very fundamental. They can easily accommodate this setting. They often read the thoughts of the students in class and the instructor. They are very discrete to not plant too many images of themselves that might betray them. Sometimes they do get some stares and looks from certain students.

Some human beings do pick up on unusual things. They might not want to admit to the implications of their intuition to themselves. Steve had an incident. I think he was at a grocery store. I think it was the cashier, where he felt that person was definitely not from here. I don't know if you have any information on that.

Humans are very intuitive to the unusual around them. They sometimes notice the 'unusual.' It depends on what is holding their focus at the time. Steve was in an electronics store looking for DVD movies and he encountered an entity that came to him that had certain striking physical features, which Steve noticed immediately. An image from the book cover of *Communion* was placed in his mind to make a psychic introduction to him. This association made it completely clear to Steve that the entity was a hybrid. Steve responded in kind with a friendly greeting, without fear, although his thoughts expressed astonishment. The hybrid appreciated the friendly greeting. Others around them were scarcely aware. He was a tall hybrid in a customer service employee uniform. He blended well into the store culture. The other employees, however, were not aware of him. He must have been able to project into these other employees (some) signals to accept him and that he was a part of them, which is not too difficult for hybrids. The hybrids use many telepathic abilities. Humans do not often consciously think of aliens. This is a great tool to manipulate their sense of reality around them. It is very effective in enabling hybrids to integrate in their midst without much human awareness of their presence.

Of the group that we are currently with, the three males and the one female, I assume they are aware that to be part of the human culture they need to have hobbies, interests. Will they tell us about any of the interests that they display superficially, or perhaps they have some interests or hobbies that they actually enjoy?

The interest in cooking does not exist. Visitors, who regularly replenish their supplies of nutrients at home, supply their food to them. Because of this, they are rather tied to this location. Their interests in school are in studying the anthropology of the present human within the extent of their understanding of human science and comparing it to their own. There are the other off-world teachers who regularly instruct them as well. In a sense, they have two mothers and two sets of friends, both at home and on Earth. They are like many exchange students in that academic environment, but in a way, that other exchange students could never comprehend. However, in social pattern, they are really quite similar, just from a place considerably farther away. Science and human sociology are of great interest. Hybrid social behavior, by comparison, would seem rather dry and sterile. Their home is rather sparse and empty. Certain posters of rock bands and others appear in the home, but this more to conceal themselves. The posters are not really of interest. It is more to put up the appearance of being human, creating camouflage.

Part of this process of integration would mean that, at least superficial, they would make friends with humans, maybe have them to their house, or go over the humans' houses. How do they deal with this?

The female has certain male human callers. She is considered attractive to humans, if in some ways perhaps a strange way. This elicits certain sexual curiosity from the male humans as well. Perhaps her natural distancing from others is interpreted as aloofness, which attracts further. The landlord is very happy with these hybrids as tenants. They do not cause trouble and the house is always immaculate. The landlord does not seem to be of much concern about them, as long as he is paid regularly. How he is being paid seems to be a mystery. They seem to have a certain account where they can draw money from regularly that seems to be readily available to them so they can pay such necessary things in human society and economy.

An average human, especially at that young age, would have a sense of competition that they express through sports or they might compete in earning grades, or compete for attention from the opposite sex. I believe that competition is not a part of your culture. How do they deal with that?

They recognize the instinctual reproductive behavior in their study of human society. They try to mimic this and at the same time, they feel it unnecessary. Sometimes the human response to this is curious. The more they may appear cold and distant, the more attractive they might inadvertently appear to humans. This is a curious human behavior that perplexes hybrids. Answers come so easily for them. Their main focus is social integration. That is their challenge. There is an added stress involved. How to integrate into human culture without becoming too human. The challenge is in not denying the other part of their heritage, which is off-world. This is part of the challenge of the whole hybrid program. It is what I would call having dual identities.

Yes. Dual identities exist for some humans, but not to the same extent. For instance, if one was an American Indian, but also an American citizen, that would be a dual identity. In terms of aloofness and the young woman, when you combine aloofness with attractiveness, it spurs interest in competition. Her perception is correct that her aloofness can intensify interest from males.

They have noticed this. Also, the human part of them, biological and emotional, is not diminished. They are dealing with new emotions and drives. The human part cannot be denied in this duality. Their intelligence accepts this duality, but there is an emotional price that cannot be repressed. This causes conflicts dealing with the duality. They both know and enjoy their duty or purpose for integrating into society. At the same time, they also miss being with a society of ones like themselves and the comfort it brings. They also miss the home that they believe is their origin. They sometimes miss home. They do not feel a part of this Earth world.

Is it part of their assignment to remain here for a long, long time?

Their exposure is remembered, downloaded, and integrated into the larger context of the human contact picture.

Wouldn't they live longer than the normal human would?

Because they do live much longer, a point comes where they have to move often and leave one society and begin again at a different location. This is because, in any long-term contact, or relationship, every human will be aging around them, and they will still look young. It will begin to betray their identity.

Because of that, does that preclude their ever having or creating families with humans?

They are experimenting with that as part of their human social studies. Some excel and some have difficulty. At some point, the human mind adapts and, in a loving way, becomes accepting of many relationships that form. Certain peculiarities are ignored because, in the process of fulfilling their own human needs, they compromise to accept the relationship. They know that one day they will grow older and the hybrid will still be relatively young. The hybrid's health and diet create a certain detachment from other institutions, such as facilities for obtaining a driver's license or health care. The health care is provided off-world, which means that there is a certain disconnect with keeping records of hybrids in human society, including a separation from legal systems and government. It is a very complex interrelationship.

Yes. I am beginning to see that.

It requires some time to accomplish this and it is not without difficulty. However, because humans are Earth-centered, humans do not consciously think in social relationships beyond their own world anyway. This helps the hybrids to blend into human society, too. Most human expectations of what an 'alien' may be are based on their own limited human cultural understanding.

Would you please thank them for allowing us to get a little glimpse of their world and a deeper appreciation for their difficulties?

They are in different locations. The female is with a human male. Two others are studying in their home and the other is in a market place, observing. Yet, they are aware of our conversation. They are very touched by being contacted by an entity similar to themselves that understands and appreciates their presence and understands the kinship. They are moving on and continuing with their duality.

Has your species ever terraformed anything on this Earth?

Not directly. You could consider, in a very rudimentary, superficial way, the consciousness planted in human society as a kind of 'terraforming.' They refer to it as the environmental movement done mainly for conservation, rather than transformation. In a very superficial form, it might be considered as such in that context. In a direct way, however, no, but in an indirect way, yes.

I had a question about a tube device at S-4. You discussed the uses of some devices at S-4 and the tube device was one of them.

We talked about the cube device and the tilting device that we had concerns about.

Perhaps I misunderstood and was hearing 'tube' device when it was really the 'cube' device.

The cube device was our concern. It facilitates a doorway to other dimensions and other timelines. It has been used as a bargaining tool by other species in exchange for permission by certain governmental authorities to permit their species to clandestinely abduct certain humans for their specie's own needs or curiosity. This was a deception by this species because the cube can be taken back at any time. It is like giving a child a toy to preoccupy their attention while the thief ransacks the house. I feel this species is deceptive about its own agendas, which we watch very carefully. We often stand in between to see that certain boundaries are not abused.

That might be the answer to the question I was about to ask, Why haven't non-Earth interests destroyed the human species already? It sounds like your sentinel stance prevents this.

We are here to protect. Also, in the context of other worlds, this is part of our political posture in relation to these other entities. The Earth has reason to stand up and exist on its own accord, but, at the same time, there are entities that see the Earth as very valuable for harvesting. There is no apparent wish to take over the Earth or control it. If they did, we would stop them before the Earth would even be aware of it.

I find it ironic that humans are so upset about being genetically sampled and harvested when, in fact, we do the same thing to other human beings and animals for research.

This is true. Like in many human relations we have known, it is all a question of context in how humans see themselves. In a larger context, they are one of many. Within their context, they see themselves as isolated. It is their human, Earth-based view, perhaps combined with a sense of pride that determines how they relate to other life forms. This is understandable in the context of their very limited perspective. Others species do not see that, but that is because they enjoy a much broader perspective that their evolution and technology makes possible. Humans do not yet have this broader perspective.

Was there ever a landing at the Holloman Air Force Base where a large number of personnel were aware of the landing?

In the 1960s there was a contact made at Holloman Air Force Base. It was very secret. It was the initial step that created many of the activities between humans and aliens now at S-4. It provided the pathway for these activities. Some political arrangements were made. Humans really had very little to nothing with which to bargain. The aliens were very much restrained by outside pressures. We were observing and were very aware of their advanced capabilities. The initial contacts were made to establish an understanding. The initial contacts to prepare for this meeting were done through a number of government contacts through hybrids and through telepathic contact. These initial contacts were not readily accepted or understood. Eventually, they were gathered together to form a convention between humans and some species. This involved meeting face-to-face at Holloman, in great secrecy.

We are aware that it was quickly covered up. Did you ever receive any information on the scientist known as Dean Judd? He was the science advisor to one of our presidents and was very much interested in the possibility of life on other planets.

There are a number of scientists who are retained as advisors to the presidents. Some presidents are fully aware of Holloman and Roswell. Some are not. It depends on the compartmentalization and the secrecy that humans often use in controlling their secrets. Judd was one who was an advisor to the President, among others retained in case certain encounters were made where further government interests may require answers. Some presidents have been aware of alien contact. A few have deliberately not been informed. However, the information was there, if later the need were to arise where it was more efficient for the President to be informed. Some knew from the beginning before they even entered presidential office due to their access to very secret information. This has been kept from the public in the day-to-day activities of the President. This is not a major concern. It is usually knowledge that is held in the background. Many of the contacts exist in such a way that any government or military influence would be inconsequential. There is little they can do to stop the action or to prevent something. Still, the President often wishes to be aware of certain events and these advisors facilitate this.

I am going to be taking a new case and her name is Cindy (pseudonym). She had an experience in August of 2003. She heard something, went outside into her backyard, and saw someone on the ground, trying to get up. Her memory is fragmented during the 40 minutes that she watched this entity. She said the entity made a chattering, cat-like sound. The most peculiar thing is that she talked about 'lights' coming out of the orifices and cracks of the entity, including the eyes. She said she heard a screeching sound. She wants me to regress her concerning this. She has had multiple sightings, including seeing a cigar-shaped craft. She thinks it might have been the same craft coming back, but this one was noisy. That was different. She said one of the events occurred the same time that there was a blackout on the East Coast. She complained about soreness in her nose that moved from one side to the other. The same condition also affected her son. Do you have any knowledge about these events?

The entity was in an injured state. She perceived the radiating energy coming out of the entity as light. It was actually telepathy, manifesting in her mind the great distress this entity was feeling, vulnerable and in fear for its life. This is a normal reaction that telepathic beings use. The witness inadvertently discovered this. Much bioluminescent life in your oceans will emit light, instinctively sending out an alarm. This being was in distress. Having been discovered, it was emitting a telepathic scream for help. In such states of extreme stress, it can show up telepathically as light in the minds of others near them. The being feared for its life. Normally, a human would never notice or understand these kinds of energies that are emitted in extreme circumstances. It wasn't actually light the witness saw, but her mind interpreted the extreme agitated energy from the being as light. This being had become injured, and in her curiosity, she approached. She felt compassion, fear, and confusion. We knew this from the resonance that permeates the wake of this event. The blackout may have been associated with this entities' craft interceding in a rescue. The missing time the witness noticed could be due to a failure to completely erase her memory of the experience. In their haste, a full erasure was not effective. Many of the memories still exist in her consciously. This is evident just from your description.

Is she strong enough to permit a regression?

Yes. Many times the experiences in human minds will loom larger, over time, in their imagination, though the event itself is not to be diminished. It is the nature of human memory to often embellish memories. Your regression will help refocus clarity on what happened, and what did not happen. It will be one that will be successful and will help her in coping with those memories. In the time since the event, she has been clouded with many other facts and circumstances surrounding it, which often magnify the context of the event itself. The event has caused some stress for her. Her other stresses have been from human interaction, and disappointment in failing to find the answers that she seeks.

Was her son also taken?

Yes. This was done in a comprehensive fashion. This is not unusual. I hope this knowledge will help you. Your contribution is part of the process. We have talked about this earlier. You are an ally in this entire process. Your part is often collecting the emotional pieces where contact between species has not been fully successful. You are involved directly in the healing process of that encounter. We apologize for the damage that comes from human misunderstanding. The regression will put everything in its proper context. It will greatly reduce the anxiety this person may feel and for those who are concerned for her.

As you have learned, the human mind greatly magnifies something that is different, and the magnification is often way beyond the importance of the event.

Human memory has that ability and we have noticed this. You have pinpointed exactly what I was ineffectively trying to convey. You have expressed my thought more efficiently. Thank you.

The Universe

No questions in this session.

Other

As you are probably aware, I work a little bit with energy by pulling it in and sending it out to those in need of healing. Would there be any opportunity for me to learn to do this a little bit more effectively and wisely? (This therapist works with subtle energies to assist in the healing process.)

Projecting healing energy?

Yes. Pulling it in and projecting it out. I know that 'intention' is the major factor for us.

Part of this is to focus on what is to be healed. At the same time, it is to draw energy from around you so you do not drain yourself. This will supplement your good gifts so that you do not deprive yourself of the same positive energies. It is like a funnel to draw in from surrounding energies and to adapt and focus these energies directed at a particular subject to be healed.

That is where the question lies because I will often pull energy and create an energy ball, but I do not direct it at a specific person or condition all the time. Rather, I ask that it be taken to where it is needed. Is this effective or am I diluting the process?

Part of it is your human nature. It does not fully understand the ailment to be healed. You understand it intellectually. This is not your fault. This is due to the typical patient being unable to express to the healer the full extent to provide a proper diagnosis and treatment. In spite of this, energy, in a physical and spiritual way, can be focused to remedy the ailment. I can sense in Steve, for example, where energy has been focused upon him and he has consciously noticed the many positive thoughts and energies that have made him buoyant and allowed him to be useful and enjoy life. He is aware of these focuses. I am sure others, too, would feel this from you. Your abilities are good. You will improve as you grow. You are well aware of the energies that you initially gather for healing, and that is the major important step. In focusing, do not doubt your abilities. Sometimes patients take time to heal. Be gratified in knowing that you are focusing the energies, and this is effective. Sometimes repeated treatments just take time to make the change that is being sought. You are effective. Sometimes healing does not occur immediately.

Open Session for Comments or Questions

Is there anything that you would like to say in closing?

No, not at this time. I am sorry for Steve's long induction and his difficulty in stepping back. He wishes me to say this. He appreciates and marvels at this process.

This is so good for him.

Yes. He feels so, too. I also feel this. It is good for all of us. There is an intimacy. Intellectually, it is one that is both stimulating and soothing at the same time. There is a resonance between us that might surprise some of my species with whom you are in contact. It gives me pleasure, if that is the correct emotion, to enjoy these contacts. It has been my main purpose for existence to create understanding between species. That is why I was selected to be a servant for you today and for my own species.

Then, for all of us who serve, I thank you, until we meet again.

Session XV, Comas, Genetic Switches, Zetans vs. Humans
November 6, 2011

Steve was inducted and went easily into a deep state. Han was invited to step forward. After a brief pause, Han says,

I am here. I am happy to be here again with you.

Steve and I are happy to have you here.

He is content. Steve is feeling like he is sleeping in a little boat and you have just pushed him away from shore. A little push and off he goes.

Earth History

You are familiar with Caracas, Venezuela. We have found a number of skeletal remains, with particularly elongated skulls. Could you tell us what you know about these skulls, whether they are human, hybrids, or something else?

These skulls are a combination of cultural influences and extraterrestrial ones. The elongated skulls were often formed in humans by wrapping the skulls of young ones while the skull structures were growing to form a unique shape to mimic the origin of this concept. Entities have often visited these cultures and humans wish to mimic this.

Is it simply humans mimicking or are there also genetic changes?

There is genetic material from off-world.

You are familiar with individuals who have gone into comas. I am not speaking of hibernation, but a coma, induced medically or by trauma. Where does the human mind go or what does it do during these times when a coma goes on for months at a time?

The human mind, as many minds do, ours included, has created places of safety, of solitude, where it preserves itself. Due to its natural ability to survive, even its consciousness places itself in a location for safekeeping. This is the mind's way of preserving itself, awaiting a time when it can be unlocked again. In a coma, the brain has shut down certain functions until the other elements of the body and mind have restored themselves. Until those other elements are healed and brought into unity and harmony as before, the elements that remain are put in safekeeping.

I know a woman who sometimes work with people who are in coma states. She has the ability to communicate with them. Sometimes, if it is appropriate, she will invite them to come out of their coma. This does not seem to be medical. It seems to be more a spiritual communication. Do you know anything about this?

In most human experience, we tend to look at the human mind in one perspective, but there are many other elements: spiritual, emotional, memory, instinctual, intellectual. There are parts that, at the appropriate time, will re-emerge, if the mind perceives that it is a safe time to do so. There is an illusion that, in a coma, some level of awareness has been lost, but there are other elements that are quite active. The human mind is always acting in a complex way. We have understood this from our contacts and have often used this to work with individuals in placing thoughts or planting ideas or memories that soothe and heal. The brain is a complex organ. It is a painter's palette with many colors that can create marvelous paintings of consciousness. This is what makes each of us who we are. In this state of coma, these elements are being saved for a future time when physiological conditions are right. I hope I am not being too abstract.

Following a discussion of the Zeta Reticulians' ability to turn off and on genetic switches to restore missing limbs, the therapist states, ' I would think that humans must also have those switches. We don't know how to turn them on and off.'

You will know, someday.

I believe it must be in our genetic codes somewhere.

Ninety per cent of your DNA is still untapped and un-explored. You are in store for some pleasant surprises.

When I say a 'pattern recognition system,' I am referring to the human ability to look at chaos and assign meaning within that chaos. It is an aspect of the survival instinct to be able to pick out faces or ears, or anything along that line. Do you also have a highly developed pattern recognition system?

Yes. This is instinctual for all intelligent beings to sort patterns for recognition of threats in survival instincts. These develop and become more sophisticated. We, with a higher degree, can interpret more complex patterns. Humans also have this ability, perhaps not to the same degree. We often observe very complex problems by your measure, which we do not see as insurmountable.

We seem to be born with it. Children start to see meaningful shapes in clouds at a very early age.

Human inkblot tests in the skies.

(Therapist laughs.) That is a good example, exactly.

This is a very human quality that combines past memories and experiences in pattern association with imagination.

You, of course, know about our scientific method.

Yes. It is a method that we also embrace.

I also find that it seems to have a corner missing. I can appreciate the methods of observation and repeatability. I instinctively know that there is an element missing that is perhaps limiting ways of exploring. Can you tell me what we might be missing?

In every scientific community, yours, as well as ours, there are certain dogmas. Perhaps this may be a surprise to you. Our own dogmas may be less defined in a broader perspective of the Universe because of our ability to travel, see, observe, and test theories that you do not yet have the ability to test. You have the apparatus to apply the scientific method. To a great degree, you lack many opportunities to test beyond the Earth. With that sense of perspective, science must consider imagination more important than information. Each serves the other. It is important to have an open and broad mind for new perspectives. Earth science has been confined to many principles that they feel are the correct ones. This has often been frustrating in our contacts with humans due to their Earth-centered mindset. It is like trying to teach a new song on a piano. It is the same music, but we have added many more notes and range to the same music, which the student does not believe is possible to play. I hope that is a good example of how much humans need to be open to new ideas and new possibilities that we practice and use continuously. What is an almost incomprehensible theory to you, we commonly use in our day-to-day lives. With each new bit of knowledge comes two or more questions. That is how science should be, changing, testing, modifying, rejecting, and replacing old knowledge with new knowledge. In recent times, human science has at least begun to consider bolder concepts.

I suspect that, because we put large sums of money up for research of specific scientific theories, it is harder to pursue many new ideas, due to the financial aspect.

Your academic structure is tied to this and this can be confining.

Oh, yes.

Only the most certain, the most hopeful research requests are given the funding for exploration. Under the circumstances, this is how we would behave, too. However, ours is not as confined. We have greater resources. We have energies and abilities that make research and study less encumbered.

Zeta Reticuli History

If one of your species dies young, what is the outside resuscitation time that you would have before you would no longer want to resuscitate that individual?

Life and death, in physical terms, is a very broad and undefined situation. I spoke earlier of how we can control our autonomic reflexes to slow down our metabolic rates. We do this for many reasons, some for survival. Perhaps this can be interpreted as hibernation, or a near death experience, but the energy of life still radiates softly from such individuals. A point will come when the mind no longer functions and ceases to exist and stops.

Are you speaking of the mind or the brain?

The brain. In our beliefs, the mind continues on in another form, along with the soul. When the physical brain ceases to function, that is our definition of when life ceases.

That is also the same definition we use, when the brain no longer functions.

We are not dissimilar in this. The suffering is not in the being whose life is departed, but in the survivors and the loved ones who remain behind. It is often they who feel the most pain.

If, after brain death, the soul in one of your species has already departed to another dimension, can you still revive the body and call the soul back?

Yes. This is possible, within certain parameters. Our medical sciences make this possible.

Are you speaking of hours or days?

A human day. In human time, usually hours, but it is not unprecedented for a day to pass. The telepathic abilities of our species can discern very clearly the separation point to beyond. Some have this specialty to communicate with souls in the other dimensions. At times, it is discerned and interpreted that these souls no longer wish to return. We respect these wishes, even though, physically, our science has the ability, to a degree, to restore them.

Our scientists are also spiritually telepathic and they realize the soul no longer wishes to return and wishes to carry on its existence on a higher plane. Our physicians have great spiritual insights beyond their desire to preserve and save lives. They are great mediators of the process of life. They see life in extraordinary terms, which they often share with the community of mind and our society. This creates a great and deep sense of contentment and peace with less fear of death, when that time eventually comes for all living things.

If your species were to lose a hand or foot would you regenerate that limb?

Yes. This is well-accepted procedure and has been a medical ability we have had for some time.

Is that a medical ability rather than a genetic ability?

It is a combination of both, genetics stimulated by the medical ability. We know the switches to turn on and off to activate the existing natural ability.

What are the primary building blocks, of say, the three or four largest components of science and does one of those components include 'consciousness?'

Yes. These are the Science of the Mind, Science of the Stars (Physics), which includes the ability to travel between stars, which relates to our physics, and the Science of Biology of our world and other worlds. Those are the three primary building blocks. Mind is an essential one, for both the health and welfare of the individual. However, it has greater importance in a telepathic society where the understanding for the health of the whole can be accessed. Through the understanding of consciousness, the mind is considered one of the three pillars you have suggested. This is true. Our sciences consist of:

THREE BUILDING BLOCKS OF SCIENCE

> The Mind
> The Physics of the Stars
> Biology

Then, what we might call the 'animal kingdom' would fall under your biology. We also have what we can describe as a 'mineral kingdom.' How would that fit into your pillars of science?

This would be in incorporated into the physics pillar. Mineral elements and compounds have been created through the factories we call stars. This also includes us, you and me, who are ultimately made from similar materials.

Then, because we are made from the same material, I would think that consciousness, in some form, would be attached to all of these things. If that is true, then a mineral would also have a form of consciousness. Is that correct?

Minerals can reflect resonating consciousness. They do not have consciousness themselves. It requires more complex combinations of mineral compounds to create a consciousness that can become self-aware. In its basic form, each compound does not have consciousness. It resonates and reflects it, but, in combination. A special, remarkable 'something' occurs and consciousness is formed. This is called the 'spark of life.'

One of the mysteries.

These mysteries are common everywhere. It is not unique to this place Earth. It is the same set of laws of physics and consciousness that exist throughout the Universe. We see these ourselves. We have observed this consistency in the Universe.

Seeing the consistency does help underscore the idea of laws of physics having some universal application.

The ability to communicate at a sub-quantum level makes it possible for such resonance to be transmitted across the Universe between life forms. This is one example of this uniformity, at least to the extent of our own understanding of the physical Universe. This is at least what we see from our larger viewpoint, looking into the past, present and future. However, even our viewpoint is limited, compared to the vast Universe and beyond. We have obviously traveled much more than humans. We have been to many places and seen many more marvels. Your physics and our physics are the same. This is universal. A feather and a stone fall at the same rate on Earth as they do on Zeta Reticuli.

I know your species travels extensively.

We love to travel.

What are you thinking when you come across something that is entirely unknown? What are the initial thoughts when you encounter something interesting and unknown?

We approach cautiously, as would any species in coming in contact with the unknown. We weigh the risk versus the benefit. We have learned that risk is necessary to acquire knowledge. At times, it may result in loss of life. It is dependent upon what price we are willing to pay for the potential benefits, whether that would be knowledge or survival. In travel to your distant moon, you learned to work as one toward a goal and accepted the risks. You knew that the benefits would be worth the risk, both for your science and for your instinctual spirituality. This also applies to us in exploring many worlds. We can martial many more resources to expand an area of exploration. Sometimes we encounter situations that confound us. With time, we learn.

We humans color our memories and change our memories to maintain our self-esteem. Does your species also do this?

This is a complex question. It is more complex than perhaps realized. There are memories that humans sometimes feel are best not remembered. Our species tends to remember the accumulative memories rather than certain points in memory quality. We look at the quantity of memories and look at the quantity in proportion to the whole. Some memories are interlaced with the memories of others of our species, as we relate to each other through our minds. In communication by thoughts, many perspectives and many viewpoints are intermixed telepathically. What one individual remembers, locked inside the human mind, can be released, and shared among others in the same species where there is such a mixture of different viewpoints. *When the individual viewpoint is viewed by others, it creates a different perspective. What may be a terrible memory for one may be seen differently when viewed by multiple minds.* Often, a memory in a human is locked inside in its own isolated pocket, either to fester or to flourish. The dynamics are different in a telepathic world, and there is a natural supportive healing that comes within the community where the need to repress unpleasant memories is less necessary. I hope this is understood.

You have emotional support groups. Imagine a support group of an entirely aware society. Perhaps humans would look at our telepathic society as a loss of individuality, but it also has many great strengths.

Yes. I am beginning to appreciate this. If we look at the overall picture of a society, I would think the goal would be to bring individuals into a state of harmony, with room for some deviations. Viewing memories with different perspectives and support would certainly be a good thing.

There is a harmony and universality. There is a sense of group consciousness where, if the individual seems diminished, each individual also grows in strength from the whole, often creating the illusion of a sum greater than its parts. This is often what makes the individual entity feel more buoyant and supported. The greater of the whole creates this feeling, yet the individual can still have his own thoughts, emotions, and feelings. These are not diminished. These are only magnified in the context of the others, which creates a deep and lasting bond between individuals in our society. This creates a peace and harmony. This is why our worlds lack war. There is understanding and a feeling that any problem encountered will be overcome because everyone understands and works toward the same solution. Each contributes. No one is deprived of this contribution. Each gives the other a sense of well-being.

Spirituality

You, personally, do you have memories of other lives that you may have lived?

I see a green place, very rich, warm, and pleasant. I feel sometimes, maybe, this was a past time in my earlier life. I see a place of beauty that I have often speculated was a time when life was simpler and my role as a facilitator and communicator with other species was not so. I imagine being in another role in our society, in our world. I often see myself as a caretaker of the land instead of as a representative. Humans would define this as a caretaker, perhaps like a farmer. This amuses me and pleases me, too. These fleeting thoughts have often been on my mind.

Those are very beautiful thoughts. Humans have similar kinds of recollections.

The chemistry of our brains is carbon-based and we have similar chemistries. Perhaps our sharing of such concepts is not so different. Perhaps our minds are more developed, but there are species that are more developed than we are. Each has respect for each other.

We share many things that would not surprise someone who is also well traveled. That knowledge brings a feeling of warmth and satisfaction that our communication and communication with other species, too, has that same fundamental bond.

Contact

May I ask you some questions about three different events? I will call them abductions.

Yes. I understand the term and its meaning.

Do you understand that when I use the term 'abduction' that is not necessarily with the same meaning that someone else might intend? You know, of course, the case of Betty and Barney Hill. The question is about an incident where she found her missing earrings in a pile of leaves on a table. She thinks those earrings disappeared during the first time she was taken. Do you have any information on the recovery of the earrings?

The entities involved were very interested in Betty and Barney. They would be considered, in a way, good aliens by your definition. They were attracted to Betty for several reasons: Her biology and her social attitudes. One reflection of this was her marriage to Barney and the curious racial situation in which she defied the conventional norm. We found this very interesting. Sometimes entities will take certain artifacts and examine them. Her earrings were one such item. Barney's dentures were another. These earrings were returned to them while they were absent from their home, many days later. It was done in a fashion like a friend might leave behind certain calling cards that only they would recognize. This calling card was a pile of leaves and a peculiar setting which Betty and Barney would recognize immediately and understand the significance. In consideration to them, her property was returned.

She was monitored throughout her life and the entities had affection for her. Their relationship was of a broader significance than she realized. Many of their memories were effectively blocked, but there was more than one visit to her and Barney. There was the suggestion in the Stanton Friedman and Kathleen Marden book, of which we are aware, that perhaps Barney was being punished for revealing their experience. This is not the case.

Unfortunately, Barney's particular physiology was such that he suffered a stroke early in his life. This was more a consequence of his physiology and medical history than anything done by these entities.

There was great sadness when Barney passed away and there was a craft present, which Betty saw when she visited Barney's grave. They stood in the background, the entities monitoring and paying their respects. Their contact was groundbreaking. Contact was then made with other humans, both in the past and in the future, after that initial contact. The Hills were one of the first. There have been earlier and later abductions by your linear timeline, but space travel, as we know it, is by its nature, also travel through time. From that first contact, all parties involved gained much experience and knowledge. Memories and suggestions implanted then were successful in beginning a carefully designed new public awareness. We wished for public awareness in the secret 1960 Holloman Air Force Base meeting, but it was denied.

The next question is about Leslie and her husband Spencer. We have been working on a case involving these people.

We are familiar with this, partially through Steve's memories.

Yes. Leslie believes that she has been visited quite recently in her current home. Do you know whether that is true?

They are being visited. At this stage in their lives they are being cared for or watched over. They are considered legacies, due to their earlier contacts. These contacts are never forgotten. In this particular case, there was some difficulty with Leslie's implants. The signals were not clear. There was also residual data coming in concerning her safety and the safety of Spencer. Spencer is quite ill. We can intercede, but only within a policy of non-interference.

Knowing the normal span of human life, we must not interfere with this process. Spencer is of concern, as is Leslie. Their lives have been disrupted in a personal and emotional way. They have not always been at peace. Life has been difficult by their standards.

We feel, and the other entities feel, a sense of obligation. It was decided to not disrupt them at this late stage in their lives. There are other legacies, who are sometimes monitored, after serving the purpose for these entities. The entities involved were a taller form of grey, with shorter greys acting as artificial biological servants. Leslie and Spencer are being watched with concern for their safety. Humans can be careless sometimes, in their day-to-day lives. We are not guardian angels. If we see something, we might intercede. Intercession was done with their safety in mind. It also presented an opportunity for other discretely performed examinations. Leslie has learned, though some of her memories have been blocked, telltale patterns of previous visits. Her suspicions, now accepted, are correct.

I don't intend to unlock those memories for her. Her attitude now is rather happy.

We agree. The memory blocks have been reinforced. In a way, much like your human surgeries, the anesthesia has been increased to compensate for any emotional pain. She has found some contentment in her later life. Her concern for Spencer is a big concern. It is part of the human cycle and we know that life is fragile. We appreciate their contribution.

I think that Leslie has somewhat come to terms with this.

We also feel that this is the case. Through your part in assisting greatly in their healing, a degree of acceptance has displaced their fear that some might interpret as irrational. If the full facts were known, the fear would be quite rational.

I think it was the original pain that was one of the larger factors in the experience.

She has an implant in her left nostril and, at times, it has been quite distressing with pain, along with her many physical ailments. This has caused her anxiety and has been a concern for her partner, Spencer. They have been a very close and small supportive unit for themselves. Alone in their experiences, they have dealt in their own ways with visits by entities who have come with good intentions and some with not good intentions.

Can't there be some adjustment made to that implant for Leslie so it won't hurt her anymore?

Its presence can be reduced and a block can be placed in her mind to help her ignore the pain. Soon, maybe, with another visit, this implant can be removed. At that time, she can be relieved of this burden. Memories of pleasantness can be placed in her mind to sedate her emotional being. This would alleviate more anxiety and stress. With that, at that time, she can have more peace.

The Universe

Will you take us on a very short journey now to allow Steve to glimpse another non-Earth culture, just to get a sense of the interaction, pace of living, and what is at the core of that civilization?

This can easily be arranged. I am in contact with intelligent beings in a distant, off-world ocean. This world is covered with water, not dissimilar from Earth's oceans. It is teaming with life, and there are many intelligent beings within these oceans. They follow many of the common methods for survival. Some die to nourish the others in the same continuous cycle of life. There is great diversity. Many communicate with each other through sounds. Many do so, which forms an evolutionary bridge to telepathy. There are turquoise seas and warm oceans.

What is their food source?

There is a natural food chain. Less cellular life forms are fed upon by larger, more complex life forms. It is the same as in your oceans. A point of intelligence and community organization is reached where some creatures dominate so they do not become a ready source of food for others. Instead, they learn cooperation in mutual defense. Schools of creatures do this. This is not a foreign concept. It reaches a level of intelligence that is sufficiently sophisticated to where many of them can even create tools.

Is it a saline ocean?

Yes. It is about the same PH as your planet. Many species there could live quite comfortably in certain regions of your planet's oceans. They could even have been transplanted. I see forms of dolphins, whales, large mammals, similar but different.

Do they use bioluminescence for communication or other things?

Yes. This is a common characteristic among many life forms throughout the Universe. It is for communication, mutual protection, or to signal alarm. Many of these creatures use bioluminescence to ornament themselves to attract a mate. Over time, this trait has become more successful and prevalent as one species dominates using bioluminescence, for instance. Many species adopt similar traits.

Of their offspring, how long do the offspring remain under the protection of their parents?

In one sense, they live like a central family unit, throughout their whole lives. In another sense, it is only in the beginning, as they venture out to begin their own communities.

Do they create farms under the ocean to raise something to eat?

They create animal husbandry-like farms. There is farming in a way that might surprise you. This creates a sense of organization and social structure that makes these beings stand out.

I love surprises! Would you please imprint in Steve's mind a very clear picture of the animal husbandry, some kind of farming, and perhaps what one or two of them might look like, for example, their coloring, the kind of skin they might have?

Some look similar to dolphins. I see great herds of creatures being herded by sound through the water. These are like the ancient cattle drives in your culture. Each species being herded has its own particular curiosities. These herding creatures use sound to call strays and return them to the fold. They are gathered into places where they can be collected and harvested for food.

When we record whale sounds, we use the recordings to call whales back into the water when they beach themselves. Is their system something like that?

Yes. In this case, it is herding to manage other species. It is done in concert and combination with others, working together, but these are the same sounds that are used for both herding and communication. They are not dissimilar from the activity that you described. An example is a whale life form being warned by its own species for its safety.

Other

No questions in this session.

Open Session for Comments or Questions

Is there anything that you would like to say in closing?

Steve is in a deep, deep trance. He is in a heavy mental state. He feels closeness with me (Han) right now. His sense of oneness is here. It is a deep dark place. He is fine, rest assured, but he is in deep waters. Steve appreciates his function and he is learning, with each session, his role. He has been successful and, with each session, he is a better translator and communicator. He is becoming very tired.

Thank you for these times and I look forward to another session, soon.

Session XVI, Junk DNA, Phenotypes, Typical Zetan Day
November 13, 2011

Steve was inducted. The therapist invited the being known as Han to step forward.

Steve: Han is here. I can see him. I am streaming from my third eye and he is there in the room with us. He is ready.

Thank you very much Steve. Thank you, Han.

You are welcome Mary. It is nice to be with you and Steve again.

Thank you. Steve is getting better each time.

Earth History

There is a theory that DNA is reprogrammed and influenced by words and frequencies. Does our junk DNA follow the same rules as human language? Are human languages a reflection of our DNA?

There is a certain genetic predisposition. A phenotype encompasses an organism's observable characteristics or traits such as morphology, development, biochemical, or physiological properties. An organism's behavior and the products of that behavior issue from its phenotype. Language is one such characteristic of this process. The free DNA that is not predisposed toward one specific role can be influenced by words. There is a great part of your being that is like clay. It is very malleable, but this trait is not yet well known to humans. This concept that we are discussing is less known than most. In the telepathic society, the ability to alter DNA without specific task assignments is more possible and quite prevalent. Our science employs phenotype simulations in genetic programming and evolutionary algorithms. Mature DNA in humans is not dissimilar to your early fetal DNA where the DNA has not yet been programmed. Before it has been designated for certain organs or tasks in the body, there is still a sublevel of DNA where a vast majority of the DNA is still capable of being programmed.

What about your own DNA? Has the majority of it already been programmed?

Our DNA is much the same as yours with some phenotype exceptions but, primarily, we are remarkably similar. This is also true of other species elsewhere. DNA is common and is not unique to Earth by any means. It is a widely prevalent chemical compound throughout the Universe. Our bodies are programmable, too, but maybe not to the same degree. It is maybe 90 per cent in humans, but 60 per cent in our biology, to the best of our understanding.

So, you still have lots of room.

Yes, we are malleable, too.

There is another theory about DNA. The theory says that our DNA produces magnetized miniature wormholes that permit communication outside of time and space. What do you think about this theory?

DNA does interact with a telepathic energy that interweaves with many quantum theories. DNA is one fundamental component that biologically enables some species to have telepathic abilities. This forms a bridge to many quantum physics. This provides a link to enable remote viewing and communication across space. We have special communicators who probe deeply into the reaches of the Universe with their minds, in a physical and spiritual way.

Are there events happening in our atmosphere that affect our aircraft that we do not yet know about?

There are many electrical discharges that have particular characteristics that are still unknown to you. One of these is what you might refer to as 'jumping sundogs.' There are certain plasma fields that sometimes manifest themselves in curious ways. One example is a lightning discharge in a thundercloud, which can temporarily change the electrical field above the cloud where charged ice crystals were reflecting sunlight. The new electric field quickly reorients these ice crystals to a new orientation that reflects sunlight differently. These dancing sundogs create sheets of light making the sundog appear to be jumping and dancing across the clouds.

For instance, what we might call St. Elmo's fire?

This is another one. These dancing sundogs have polarities, which reverse back and forth, creating sheets of light that reorient ice crystals back and forth like louvers. We have noticed these in navigating, not only in this world, but also in other worlds with similar atmospheres and conditions.

I can imagine that some other worlds could have quite violent atmospheres.

Many of your own atmospheric conditions can be quite violent as well. Imagine another planet, such as Jupiter. It experiences decimal points in energy values that shift by several orders of magnitude. The physics are the same, but the energy released can be astonishing.

Just the subject of electricity requires years of study.

Your Benjamin Franklin would have had quite a shock on Jupiter.

(Therapist laughs.) Well, he is on the spirit side, so maybe he has visited Jupiter.

I would not feel there is much that could contain such a soul as Benjamin Franklin, in all aspects of his life. We are aware of him.

Zeta Reticuli History

If I may ask, what would you like to tell us about yourself and your day-to-day life?

A day, for me, is different from a human day. Day and night are roughly 36 hours in duration, due to our planet's rotation facing our two suns. We only have partial nighttime. There are only certain points of the year where we have total night. Our days are longer than an Earth day. There is a period of sleep. Then there is mealtime. Then there is activity in my dwelling, where I live. My space is rather an open space. It is like a home with few walls where the landscape becomes part of the interior of the home. There is a sense of openness without being enclosed, yet I am protected from inclement weather and from night and from temperature fluctuations. This is arranged with invisible walls, where there is a building structure, but parts of it are quite open. It is much like an Eichler style home in some of your architecture on Earth. There is a sense of spaciousness and freedom. The openness is a reflection of our architectural philosophy.

Since we live in a telepathic society, the sense of privacy in an enclosure is not the same as it is in your society and the architecture unconsciously reflect this. There are spaces for meditation, food preparation, and places for guests in my home. This is typical. There are periods when I am in meditation where I am communicating with the community to learn the latest information, news, and communications. This is much like your Internet, but done through telepathic communication. At times, this communication is unconscious as we go about our activities. We also devote specific times in which we intentionally transmit and receive thoughts on a much-increased level, with a greater volume of information exchanged on many levels. At times, I will physically travel to different places on the planet. At other times, I telepathically transport my mind to other planets for communication with my species or other species, much the way that we are communicating here, now, with you.

I can see dusk setting in. My home is underground with a large swathe of openings, what would be like windows, overlooking the grounds. It looks like a large cut into the hillside where the roof is formed into the hillside and then there is a row of 'windows' and open space. I have gardens. They form the front area of these openings. The gardens overlook a valley where there is a river and mountains. The sunset is happening now, with the ocean in the distance. There are other homes in the area, too, but they are not seen, so there is the illusion that there are no homes visible when there actually are many homes. They are terraced in such a way, from your viewpoint, that the view you enjoy is exclusively yours when, in fact, it is not. This was cleverly done by our builders. This is a common practice.

There are energy sources that come to our homes and there are the usual facilities for food, energy, and comfort. There are statues in my home, slim, open, elegant statues of different shapes. These are placed very artistically around the home. The colors are a kind of rose, beige with white and turquoises and greens, and a very clean, immaculate look with sharp straight lines. There is a sense of openness, but it is not a cold openness. There is warmth that is comforting to the mind and the senses. Much of the house is free of material things. The walls and the shapes of the rooms are much more important in our architecture in how they appeal to the mind. The colors and shapes create soothing feelings or feelings of alertness, depending upon the room and the room's purpose. Some rooms have starker colors. Others have more soothing colors, again, depending upon the purpose. Rooms for sleep and meditation are very soothing. The rooms for tasks have more specific colors that appeal to the mind to devote concentration and focus. My day is then spent with my colleagues.

We share the same tasks, along with communication with my neighbors and my telepathic work in the community and off-world. There are times for meals and times for guests. I often have guests in my home. There are relationships I have with neighbors. Some are friends. Some are closer than friends.

With these, I have an intimacy in our exchange of thoughts. It is also possible to have physical intimacy. It does not necessarily require a physical presence. There are a number of relationships, on a number of levels, where each shares in the pleasures of intellectual stimulation. At the end of what would be a long day for a human, there is time for relaxation from our sense of purpose or work, and there is time for rest. Then the day begins again. That is perhaps a typical day. There is not much traveling in a physical sense. It can all be accomplished telepathically. It is much like your concept of working from home on the Internet, but in a more elaborate fashion, done telepathically. We even telepathically speak to the house. This, I hope, might be a representation of my day.

That was very generous. How is food brought to each home? Does the occupant shop outside of the home to obtain food and clothing?

Clothing serves functions in society for the different roles they play. We often do not wear clothing, as you would call it. Some of our organs and respiration require clothing that does not confine these. The food comes from a number of places. It can be grown synthetically at home. Frequently, our food is delivered from farms. We can visit the farms. There are centers, where foods from different areas of the planets, what you call markets, exist where we can bring home these nutrients for ourselves for the enjoyment of them.

I have the feeling that you do not have an economy in a human sense, but perhaps have a kind of cooperative, a trading of services. Is that how you obtain goods?

It would be very socialistic by your standards. Politically, there is a sense of trade and exchange. It creates a uniformity that, in a telepathic society, would be consistent with that in a physical sense. There are no rich or poor, just standardization. The individual's dwelling where they live can express the individual's tastes. At the same time, there is uniformity. Ambitions do exist and we wish to be successful in an intellectual sense in the sciences and in new thought and scientific discoveries. That is the main drive for us. It is not, in fact, an economic drive.

In our economic structure there is no money in the sense that you use money. However, there is a value placed on things in a different sense. It is hard to explain. My skills are focused on diplomacy, communication, and less on economics. We do have a sense of economics and a system. This is necessary to interact in trade with other planets. Therefore, it is necessary, on a broad scale, that such a system exists. On an individual level, it is more diffuse and less noticeable. There is just a sense of abundance and a sense of no need or want. This is telepathically translated into the economy and the physical well-being of each person. This is rather abstract and it is not my particular skill set.

That is all right. It is good for both of us to stretch in different directions. That is what makes these meetings interesting.

I am glad to be able to be of service.

If you had a guest become ill, would you call in a physician or would you take that person to a place that would be akin to a hospital?

In your society, in such a situation, you may take someone to such a facility earlier than we would. Much of the knowledge and healing energy can be imparted to us remotely and collectively to deal with that situation for ourselves. We can transform our minds to become doctors on the spot for healing or whatever soothing or skills are needed. These are transferable. There are, however, certain physical skills that require manual dexterity and experience, which certain others have practiced. For example, we can transfer the knowledge of music and apply an appreciation of it, but to play certain music, to use that analogy, would require certain skills. In a medical emergency we would apply many treatments. After that, if necessary, the sick individual would be taken to a certain facility where they would continue treatment from there. The need and number of doctors, as you would refer to them, are fewer, but medical knowledge, healing, and certain skills can be imparted upon the general public, freely and ostensibly, to remedy most ailments. Some of the more acute ailments require special skills and dexterity, which, at that point, the public remedies would step aside and the specialists would step in.

If you do not mind my asking, to what extent does your species use its mind to move material objects?

There are several levels to the answer to your question. There is a psychotronic ability, which we have. In the craft that humans sometimes see that we are associated with, this is an example of technology where our minds and the spacecraft or time craft (they are synonymous) can be an extension of the mind. Humans have known this. When humans fly aircraft, we can sense in their minds when the machine becomes an extension of the human body. This occurs with craft that has well-constructed and designed physical apparatus. In a real physical sense, the psychotronic ability is how we very commonly operate our own craft or our technology on our worlds.

There is also another layer where there are no psychotronic connections at the receiving end. The human or alien mind can manipulate matter to transform it to levitate or manipulate a change. This is done through the powerful abilities of some minds to focus energies and resonating forces. We cannot move mountains, but we can move many stones and similar objects.

Is this primarily in a group situation?

No. Certain individuals of our species can do this. With more minds, they can create even more. This is true.

Yes. We do have a few people who can move objects with their minds.

There are many ways both our species and the human species can move things and touch others, physically, mentally and emotionally. We often send out waves, which affect others, that can ultimately extend into infinity.

We have learned to use mass thought to bring rain.

I encourage you as students to take stock in the progress you have made. You are further along than maybe you realize.

As you said, for every question that is answered, at least two more questions form. I see how this process is beginning to open us up, both Steve and myself.

You are a philosopher.

I had a mother who taught me to be curious and to love life.

Your mother is loving you now. She is expressing her thoughts with yours. You are both your own individual selves and you are the sum of both you and your mother.

It makes me very happy to know that she can now pursue all those things that she could not pursue while in physical form.

She is happy in that. You have become the intellectual hands for her, as well as for yourself. Your thoughts are your own, but know that her touch is in those hands, too.

Spirituality

I doubt that you have this condition in your society, but here on Earth, we sometimes have babies born who are Siamese twins in that they are conjoined. My question is actually about their higher selves, or their souls or their minds. I would think that they would have separate souls, but I am not sure since they are genetically so linked. What do you think about that?

That is an interesting question. There are a number of species on planets who would be considered 'Siamese.' These issues and questions have been brought up before. If they have individual minds, then if their genetic makeup is so conjoined, much of the knowledge and energy and spiritual consciousness emanates from the mind. The soul is conjoined with that mind. If two are linked as one, in a physical sense, literally, if they have two minds, there will then be two souls. The soul is linked to the mind in that relationship. This is what we have discovered in our experience.

On rare occasions, there have been two heads fused at the top or maybe the back where the brain was partially merged. Then, in this instance, the concept of the single mind becomes a question mark.

At that point, the mind would be joined for both bodies and they would share the same soul.

You, of course, know that human beings have a gland called the pineal gland. Some of us believe that the pineal gland is a gateway to spiritual experiences. Do you have such a gland and is it true that it is a gateway?

There are many parts of the human mind, and other places, that have glands for different purposes. These can create thoughts and instincts or motivations for protection, sexual reproduction, and for spiritual and emotionally heightened states. Also, there are glands for intellectual thought. There is much that you will learn about your own minds. One day your species will acquire telepathic abilities and a growing sense of awareness that will change the structure of your planet and your society. When that time comes, that will be an exciting day. One of these glands does perform that role in providing a spiritually heightened awareness. It is not dissimilar with us.

Do the glands excrete enzymes that move throughout the body to make chemical changes and, therefore, emotional and intellectual changes?

Yes. Primarily, the glands do this to help focus more of the brain's capacity to specific tasks. This is to augment the capacity of a specific role within the brain itself.

As you have probably become aware, I am somewhat mediumistic and have a little knowledge of the afterlife. What would your spiritual leaders/counselors tell us about the afterlife that would surprise and comfort us?

In the afterlife, there would be an added connection with all things and the great energies that can be harnessed in that dimension that is almost difficult to comprehend. The spiritual aspect knows every falling leaf and, at the same time, can harness the energies of a black hole or a sun. This expansive consciousness that is harnessed is profound. That would be the quantum leap that characterizes the afterlife that would astonish and give one solace at the same time. It is the security of everything being connected to everything that lives forever.

First, know that there is an afterlife. Logically, that would be the first question. I have answered that. There is another dimension, a higher one of heightened spiritual and moral purpose. It is the natural inter-dimensional, inter-universal step. There are regions where the soul, as a 'vessel,' explores these seas of heightened spiritual consciousness. There is a more diffuse sense of energy where it permeates to an even deeper level of consciousness with all things and all beings. In our present physical world, the main difference would be the connection with other life forms.

Thank you. I did know that, in the spirit world, souls could create. I did not know that they could do so at such a great level. I assumed that they would go through various layers of learning before they reached the stage that you mentioned to create with such great capacity. Although I know about the existence of the afterlife, I am still astonished that we and other species have been given such a gift. That is what is beyond my understanding.

There is a force that is greater than the previous dimension it left. It is like a hand that reaches down, takes hold, and lifts the soul to the higher level, which it cannot attain by itself. It is with this force from beyond that makes this possible. It reaches to the soul, lifts it up, and brings it to the afterlife. Why that energy is greater than the previous level and how it increases in a physical universe where entropy is the norm is a great mystery to us. Instead of decreasing, the spiritual energy seems to increase.

We will continue to have these sessions. We wish you a fond goodnight.

End of Session.

Session XVII, Contact Cases, DNA
November 20, 2011

Steve was inducted.

What do you see Steve?

Steve: I can see Han. His back is turned to me and he is looking over his shoulder. He is smiling, but this is conveyed more as thought. He is getting comfortable with us. He is very happy to see us. I see this orchard in France, and we are on a hillside near a tree. There is kind of a wooden bench near the orchard. It is very weather beaten. We are sitting together. He is on one end, and you are on the other. I am watching. His hands are clasped and he is enjoying the view of the valley. It is very beautiful, southern France. Dr. Vallee comes to mind. I do not know why. Maybe it is just a thought. He is waiting for you, whenever you are ready. There is the smell of vineyards, and I feel a gentle breeze on this warm summer afternoon. We are in the cool shade.

The scene impression in my mind seems almost nonchalant. It feels like a deep discussion is about to happen. It is a sense of exchanging conversation, but giving the impression that we are only gazing out at the beautiful valley and vineyards. It is like two government employees unofficially sharing interdepartmental information at their regular weekly meeting to solve a mutual problem, yet appearing like two strangers sitting on the same park bench, casually watching the world go by.

Thank you so much, Steve, for describing the surroundings. Han announces his presence.

Mary, it is nice to be with you again. I created this setting in which to meet. I thought it would be enjoyable for both of you and Steve.

I have heard that France is very beautiful, so it is nice to be here.

It is a peaceful setting, and no one will intrude, yet we can see the world go by.

Please excuse us for changing the session time. We want to be consistent.

This is quite all right. Time is an abstract. It is the here and now and yet, it is 'every' time. Thank you.

Earth History

Where did the water on Earth come from?

The oceans are composed of the basic elements of oxygen, hydrogen, and compounds known as salts, creating a natural salinity. They originated from the very primitive atmosphere as it slowly evolved and the planet's development formed these elements and linked up to form compounds. This does not evolve overnight. Water is an abundant and common compound in the Universe, in various gaseous, solid, and liquid states. It is even on nearby planets and moons, such as Europa around Saturn. Mars has such water. There is water on many planets, including oceans. Ours, too, is an ocean planet. In the proportion of land to sea, we have more land than sea, but we do have enough to create a good balance and maintain an atmosphere quite suitable for life. Water came from these basic elements. They combined to form the water that you understand today.

Water on the young Earth came from two sources: out-gassing from within the Earth and bombardment by comets. Out gassing is the process whereby gases are released from molten rock in the mantle of the planet by volcanic activity. This was probably the primary source of gases for your early atmosphere. Comets and meteorites also bring gases with them, which contributed to the Earth's atmosphere. Some of the gases in this new atmosphere were methane, ammonia, water vapor, and carbon dioxide. The water on Earth stayed in gaseous form until the planet's surface cooled. About three-

and-a-half-billion years ago, conditions were right for water to condense into rain and poured onto the land. Water collected in low-lying areas, which gradually became the primitive oceans.

Water has many wonderful qualities, but my favorite is that water is clear and leaves no perceptible residue.

The ocean waters also provide a nursery for early life in its most primitive state. Such a large ocean is necessary. It is hard to imagine an ocean without life in its beginning. It just existed as liquid in a neutral state, but, in time, these oceans created the optimum situation for compounds to form into complex cellular life. The process of life began on this planet, as it has on others. It is a beautiful concept. This did not occur artificially. This occurred naturally and independently on its own. Even we could not create on such an extensive scale. We can terraform and transplant, but there are certain processes that we respectfully leave untouched.

Zeta Reticuli History

No questions in this session.

Spirituality

No questions in this session.

Contact

Yesterday, I regressed a woman named Cindy (pseudonym). It was difficult for her, but she finally managed to complete the process. I believe that she was able to do that. She seems happier now.

I can assure you that she is *very* happy and a great weight was lifted from her.

I am so glad.

She is relieved about herself and her son. She has a sense of completeness now. She understands more of the situation in which she was involved.

I wanted to ask you about the noise that she heard, and also to ask about how the entity may have been injured, if you know.

Cindy discovered the entity. The scene was one of great confusion and fear. Several dogs had injured the entity. The being was holding them at a distance with its mind, trying to pacify the dogs. It was focusing its mind to protect itself, telepathically holding the dogs at bay, while suppressing its own pain and fear. This requires great focus and mental discipline in a chaotic situation.

Were they neighbor dogs or Cindy's dogs?

I don't know this. There were three dogs, a pack. They were being protective and, at the same time, afraid, too, I sense.

Had the being been bitten?

Yes. It was mauled.

Oh. That would have been quite severe.

Something went wrong. An invisible energy barrier that usually envelopes such entities from human bullets, weapons, or harm had failed and the dogs noticed the being. The being felt invulnerable, but something went wrong. The dogs attacked. The dog sounds attracted Cindy. The entity suddenly realized the passive field protecting it had become ineffective. The entity was able to save himself from further damage, but was injured and unable to move well enough to escape. He was using his mind to call out for help and to push the dogs back.

Cindy felt great compassion and sorrow for his injuries.

She was horrified, stunned, compassionate, and confused, and she did not know how to help. I think the entity sensed this, too. It was a scene of much energy. Almost a panic situation, but a craft quickly came and enveloped the whole scene to regain control. The rescue required retrieving the being, subduing the dogs, and taking everyone away who was conscious of the situation so there would be no memory trace. The entities did not do an effective job with this. Sounds were used to accomplish control. The sounds of a craft are mesmerizing. This is often used to pacify and take control of all of the parties being visited. The entities use this as a protection to help control anything they may not anticipate.

There were two sounds. One, I would say, was to create a state of hypnosis. It was kind of a 'whoooom, whooom, whooom' sound. The second sound was like an old truck idling, making a fair amount of noise. Was that also part of the operation?

The 'thrum' is a hypnotic effect. It affects the mind and consciousness of all the living forms within a specific area. It acts as a soothing device to pacify or sedate where people are often conscious, but they do not seem to mind what is happening. This makes them pliable, to be controlled telepathically and responsive to instructions. This is often what occurs during 'abductions.' They are conscious, but there is a certain level of unconsciousness. This 'thrum' has a limited range and within this range it enables those away from the ship to carry out their duties in relative safety. A tragedy was barely prevented.

And the second sound?

The second sound was a secondary effect of the craft. It was a growling, low, soft sound with a rhythmic pattern of higher frequency. Sound cancellation was used. This technology is not that advanced. It is basic technology for us. Even humans are learning the ability to direct sounds at specific targets. We have mastered this and so have the species who were involved with Cindy.

I make the assumption that the governments of the world are interested in telepathic communication between human beings and non-Earth beings. I assume that our government makes an effort to listen to interesting cases. Does George LoBuono still have a certain amount of privacy from governmental eavesdropping?

George is being watched, but on a level much like walking in front of a dragon. If he tiptoes, the dragon will barely open an eye to notice his presence. He does not awaken the monster that could make his life uncomfortable. It is known, he is also aware, and respects those who watch him. He is careful so that he does not cause too much notice or draw attention to himself. So far, he should have the correct level of caution, balancing awareness and taking precautions for himself and his family. They are aware, and he is aware of them, too. Both balance and there is no need by the opposing force to be more inquisitive. He is dealing with abductions, is in contact and so are his children. This is concern enough. Other governmental agencies have little ability to prevent or take consequential action in this. When entities visit, George's attitude is one of caution and openness, optimism balanced with common sense. He treats entities as one might with any stranger, welcoming, but with caution. His main concern is protection of his family. To that extent, he can only do so much. He is using a common sense approach, which is very advanced and sophisticated compared to most experiencers. He is also well-connected with other entities that also have an interest in him and are looking out for him, too. While there are some entities that might cause concern, other entities protect. This interaction is part of the greater galactic community with which he is in contact. They invited him in and made the initial contact. George responded in kind and has ever since.

Was he a child when this first happened?

He was visited, but the communication that he now experiences began in earnest later in life in his twenties and he has been a remarkable communicator and doorway between humanity and many off-world intelligences. Each has different intentions, motives, and concerns. Some of these entities are in competition. George has been made aware of the more complex off-world politics. He has been given access. You have been given access, too. Even comparing you with me, and, to a degree, Steve, George is on a galactic level of interaction between many species. George is at the forefront of this. With this come some consequences and life complications. In his mind, he is transported to a government city, where the main focus of politics is played out.

I am sorry to hear about the competition. I was hoping that evolution had removed that as a factor.

It is not an urgent competition. It is just viewpoints and ambitions, spread across thousands of years, not sharp incidents. They do not cause great conflicts. There is a sense of higher purpose and a quiet understanding that exists. Competition may be a harsh word for it. I am not finding the word I want.

Different levels of self-interest?

Yes. That is a good term.

Thank you.

Would you prepare, at your own leisure, two questions for Steve and me, either or both of us, just for the purpose of stimulating our thinking. We don't particularly want the answers at this time, but we would like to have our thinking stimulated by hearing a couple of questions that would do that.

Zestra: Han is thinking. He has been focusing on answers.

A question is, 'How will humanity solve its population explosion problem in a manner that is not self-destructive?'

Therapist's Answer: When humans find that it is more financially beneficial to limit populations, it will occur in some measure, i.e., China. Humanity is currently more driven by financial consider-

ations than altruistic considerations, or even long-term survival.

Another question is, 'When will humanity be at a place in its evolution where it will gain a telepathic social order?' It is one that we have achieved. Perhaps it is a rhetorical question that only time will reveal.

Therapist's Answer: For me the second question would not necessarily be when this would occur, but rather, what situations need to occur before the genetic code is altered in such a way that telepathy becomes common? I suspect that it will become activated when environmental factors press in that direction.

A certain turning point in the road will arrive, and, if humanity survives to that time, it will begin that journey, one that will be transformational beyond humanities' wildest dreams. It is one that will affect every living sentient being on the planet in a very deep and meaningful way. Our society may give you a glimpse of what lies ahead. Your question is framed in the proper context of what conditions would be needed for this new genesis of thought and formation of a new community of minds.

One of the very first aspects of that would be to place less emphasis on privacy and more emphasis on the greater good. I have already felt a small shift in that direction. We enjoy privacy, but we also can relinquish it for a better purpose. The illusion of privacy may start much like the allegory of your Internet. Your curiosity will lead you to greater knowledge and in turn, that knowledge will realize that it is well aware of you, too, and the privacy you cling to will then be only an illusion. A new security may come from the many. A new connection, beyond oneself, will come that will be quite profound. Many of your governments, in their present form, hold to a high standard the individuality of the human being and the desire to pursue a life of happiness and fullness. Eventually, that pursuit will link up and merge with others in a telepathic fashion and a new structure for your society will be formed.

Quite unintentionally, a technological evolution will probably become a very organic one, which will become a revolution of everything that you know. The changes that could result will be welcome ones. I can foresee greater understanding and compassion, a potential for unity or disunity on a planetary scale.

The responsibility of each will be magnified among the many. A telepathic society brings new mental and telepathic forms of courtesy, ethics, and mental discipline. This occurs when all know that their thoughts are shared. It will depend on your willingness to let go of past patterns of individually.

Socially responsible thoughts and concepts of politeness will form on a new level. Politeness will extend to the mind, knowing that the mind can now be viewed by many. This will create great fundamental changes in knowing that the very thoughts of a person will be the sum and measure of what makes a sentient being what they are. This is not in a material sense, but in an intellectual, moral, spiritual sense. The strengths and the vulnerabilities of the individuals join into the many and create a sum greater than the parts. When that time of reckoning in your evolution arrives, it will be a challenging time for humanity, but one that will stretch and provide great rewards in the end. You then will be full members of a community that dwells among the stars.

Therapist's Answer: This already exists to a smaller extent with the Aborigines. The criteria for developing the skill would be that no other long distance communication is available and survival depends upon some kind of long distance communication. The development of telepathy would be encouraged in any situation where normal communication is not possible for extended periods of time. It could also be developed solely for a need to communicate with loved ones. For example, the Aborigine's method of 'singing someone home.' Technology seems to be interfering with the development of the ability by making communication easily available. In this sense, technology is delaying the development of a telepathic community.

The Universe

I wanted to talk to you about a concept known as 'quantum resurrection,' that is the idea that a particle might spring out of nothing if one has infinite time. Does that create the possibility of the resurrection of the Universe if there were nothing? Could, in fact, a particle spring from nothing?

At the most fundamental level, this is how the Universe was partially created. Something was created from nothing. Quantum theory permits the existence of other universes to provide matter, which can issue forth, departing one universe to be transformed to create a second universe through the membranes that exist between universes at certain key intersections. It is immense to think that all matter in the Universe can come from one horizon event, but this is often how many universes are formed. However, the question still exists. Where did the first universe begin, and where did the matter from the first universe come from? That ultimate origin lives and sleeps within the strange mysteries of quantum physics.

Could it have come from thought, a thought without any physical form?

It is very conceivable. We have often discussed the ability of thought to manipulate matter and move matter. There is a connection between thought and matter in the Universe, in a quantum way, where one can transport oneself to a distant place by merely focusing thought. Such quantum physics toss out all concepts of linear time and space. This matter and form from thought would have to be a consciousness of almost omnipresent wisdom and ability. We can refer to it as many things, a superior being, or God, but maybe it is, as are many things in the Universe, a natural process that is just beyond our ability to conceptualize. In time, more wisdom and knowledge will permit an understanding of these concepts. This is another mystery that you touch on.

I had the thought that we human beings give too much validity to the physical aspect of being and keep searching for that invisible-to-visible link. I have to think that the invisible has just as much validity. Perhaps it is not necessary to be searching so hard for the transition point. This is just a thought.

When you consider the Universe and all that it encompasses, there is always more to be discovered that is not yet perceived. Your Shakespeare in his story about Hamlet stated it well, that there is more to heaven and Earth than we realize. Hamlet may teach you that science is a tool and not an answer. It evolves and changes as your understanding changes and your knowledge grows. As we attempt understanding of this consciousness, there is much more influencing what we do not see surrounding us. There are invisible forces, energies and resonances that touch us in ways that we do not always comprehend or may even be aware of. It is partly that connection that facilitates our quantum communication we are experiencing here and now. For everything we learn, there are more questions that, if answered, can give a fuller picture of the seemingly incomprehensible. I hope my words do not seem too vague.

No. I have no difficulty following you.

Good.

Are you familiar with the term 'Dyson's Sphere?'

Yes.

The way it was explained to me was it was like placing concentric circles or something like an intermittent sphere, around a star to collect energy. Is that your understanding of it?

Yes. It is a space with a structural shell surrounding this space, containing and harnessing, in a very efficient manner, all energy radiating from a star. This Dyson's sphere can contain much area for life. These are very advanced concepts for very advanced civilizations. The Dyson's sphere is one method. There are not many Dyson's spheres, but they do exist. This is a theory that some Earth theorists have correctly surmised. Some Dyson spheres, as you refer to them, can be difficult to detect in the Universe.

Well, it makes sense, on the surface. There are so many stars and tremendous energy available.

Your Russian astronomer, Nikolai Kardashev, created different categories or levels of sentient intelligence development on a scale of a solar system. A Dyson's sphere represents a very advanced civilization. We have similar classifications. *Earth, at present, does not even register on these scales.* It has yet to focus and harness energies efficiently and cooperatively on a planetary scale. The next order of magnitude could encompass such concepts as a Dyson's sphere.

I am glad to hear about the Russian astronomer's work and his interesting way of measuring societal advancements. This makes sense to me.

Our concepts are not dissimilar. Humans are beginning to conceive of advanced concepts beyond Earth that are happily not totally Earth-centered in concept.

Yes. That seems to be one of our weaknesses. We have to learn to think way outside of ourselves.

Have patience. You are advancing quickly. Humans need to be less confined in thought, use imagination freely, and give themselves permission to conceive far beyond their present concepts. This is the beauty of knowledge and imagination in harmony to conceive those thoughts. If humans could see for themselves, they would marvel how their concepts, in some places of the Universe, are expressed in various forms of reality.

Yes. Sentient beings have the gift of imagination. This sits beside telepathy in terms of usefulness and wonder.

Imagination is the glucose that fuels your body in its strenuous exercise for knowledge. It is a side effect of a sentient being's self-awareness – to know oneself, but to know there is more beyond. Curiosity is the driver. With delight, I anticipate what is yet in store for you to discover.

Other

This next question has to do with programming DNA. I know it is programmed by environmental conditions. If I hypnotize someone and work with their subconscious mind, can I enable them to see their environment in a different way that would have the effect of altering their DNA?

Hello?

Yes. I am here. Han is working on the question. Perhaps it is a larger question than I anticipated.

The question has now been presented. The question again is, 'How does environment affect DNA?'

Well, we know that DNA is altered by environmental factors.

Yes.

The question is, 'If I give a suggestion to someone's subconscious mind about their environment to perceive that environment in a different way, will that, in turn, affect or change their DNA?'

If the mind perceives its reality in one way, that perception can influence DNA. Another thought can be suggested that can create a variant form of DNA, due to the mechanism of the thought projected toward that aim. The power of a thought is of greater consequence than many realize, particularly for a telepathic species. It can influence other physical forms, such as DNA. Yes. It can be done.

Is it possible for us to take a short journey to another planet to see another civilization and the way that they live? Could it be a little different from ours so that we might learn something?

I am searching. I have wished to present a pleasant picture. However, there are also places that are less pleasant. These should be shared, too. There are many planets that have species that can be oppressive and confining, almost suffocating in the misuse of their planets. A species may follow one line of technology and before it is noticed, take it to excess. It can become very oppressive. I see planets with entire surfaces filled with lights and cities, like a planet that presents an ugly clue where life, technology, and nature are out of balance. These planets contain civilizations that are like a bright light, burning brightest before it burns out. I do not wish this for your planet. There can be inefficient uses of energies that are selfish and only benefit a few, forming an economic system that only rewards the few and not the many. There are places like this that we respect for their own path of choice, but we are happy we did not follow such a path.

Our advanced technology is a servant of our organic needs. We have never forgotten who we are, and that, ultimately, it is the well-being of all of the inhabitants of the community that is important. There are places of ugliness that offend my senses, but which you must know exist, too. I do not wish to present a totally 'rosy picture,' as you might call it.

Know that these are anomalies and that the species that survive are ones that see beyond themselves and have a sense of well-being that is one with the planets they live on and with the Universe. These are ones who respect their origins and how they ultimately became sentient beings, much like your Native Americans and the Aborigine culture in Australia where they live simply and in balance with the land. They see their source of life and strength. They live their lives, respecting the planet on which they live. Some species overbuild or overpopulate and, in their own selfishness, destroy themselves. We do not wish to emulate these places.

The Universe is a big place and not all habitats are like this. I tell you this to make you aware.

We appreciate that. All learning is not necessarily beautiful. I envision something like Hong Kong that covers an entire planet. When I see a city that does not allow trees along its streets, then I worry that they have lost touch with the planet.

They refuse either symbolically or in actuality to see the cycle of life. They do not see how a planet's life can provide the needs of others who depend upon oxygen while plant life depends upon carbon dioxide for life. When populations become so out of balance that they become oppressive, even to their own lives, they destroy, in a larger sense, what their planet can offer back. There is no longer a balance and a symbiotic relationship. We have understood this. We almost came to that precipice. Instead, we reformed our planet so that its surface provides a beautiful and vital environment.

I admire the way that you did it by building underground and allowing the surface to be a continuous green zone.

We live in harmony with our world now, with abundance for both. There is ample exchange between the organic and the technology and this creates a heightened spirituality as well.

Open Session for Comments or Questions

It is getting close to time to close the session, but I wanted to tell you how much I enjoyed the tree forms on the forest planet journey. Steve took a kind of modified journey because he was stressed. Perhaps his dreams can bring him some better things tonight. Is there anything that you wish to add at this time?

He tried his best. He was interrupted by the concerns of others, but there will be many other times. He has many dreams. Some he remembers. There are many dreams that he does not remember. Lately, I have been planting thoughts in his mind, too. Much like the cat he strokes, I will stroke his consciousness, as I have also touched yours, and will try to give knowledge with a sense of contentment. Steve is learning to become less anxious. This is a skill that you have helped both him and many others acquire. It is a special gift to relieve such anxieties. Eventually, one will find contentment in the moment, hope for the future, and warmth that comes from memories of the past. In the journey through life, we all have these similar experiences. We both share these, you and I. In your way, your services to many others mirror many of the intentions and wishes of our species, too.

We thrive in seeking peace and reflecting upon the wonder of what it is to live in the moment and to rest in that. We hope that Steve will have a life that includes even more happiness for him and for you, Mary. Zeta kin relationships all share in happiness. The one thing humans will learn is that they may one day surrender some of their individuality, but they will also surrender loneliness, and become conscious of those surrounding them. There is not so much loneliness in Steve or in you, Mary. This, again, is part of the process of growth that makes us who we are. That is all I wish to say now.

Thank you. Your feelings extended way beyond your words.

Until we meet again.

I wish you well for this week, and in your tradition of taking stock of your blessings, you have a happy holiday. I also wish this for your species. *(It is Thanksgiving week.)*

Good day and I look forward to our next meeting, at your request. I am your servant in our exchange of communication.

Thank you.

INDEX